OFF THE FENCE

OFF THE FENCE

DISABILITY ADVOCACY

Pat Linkhorn

iUniverse LLC
Bloomington

OFF THE FENCE
DISABILITY ADVOCACY

iUniverse books may be ordered through booksellers or by contacting:

iUniverse LLC
1663 Liberty Drive
Bloomington, IN 47403
www.iuniverse.com
1-800-Authors (1-800-288-4677)

ISBN: 978-1-4917-1091-3 (sc)
ISBN: 978-1-4917-1093-7 (hc)
ISBN: 978-1-4917-1092-0 (e)

Library of Congress Control Number: 2013920090

Printed in the United States of America.

iUniverse rev. date: 11/15/2013

Contents

Introduction

This is the tale of my adventures in raising two atypical children. My older daughter is autistic. We adopted her when she was about a year and a half old. She came to live with us in November, and in January of the following year, I became pregnant with our second daughter. She was born prematurely, and, as a result, is blind.

I was fortunate enough to become involved with some state and federal organizations in the early years of my children's lives. My first job was with an organization that worked with families who had children from birth to three years of age who had disabilities. I was able to receive training, network with other parents, and help new parents coming into the system find services.

My next job was mentoring parents who had children between the ages of three and twenty-one in the educational system. For twelve years, I worked with several school districts providing this service. Throughout those years, I received training and attended workshops that helped me understand the system.

I then worked with a statewide parent-training agency for four years. It was a more intense version of my previous job.

This is a story of survival and victory, as well as what all parents need to know from a viewpoint of a parent who has worked within the system as a mentor/advocate. It's not your typical manual to guide you through the special education maze. Certainly, I'll share strategies I've learned along the way. Some of it might seem like a rant against the system, and the people in it: Some of it is! Mostly, though, it's a look into how the system actually works to provide some helpful insight.

Over the years, I've learned that there are many events in the lives of parents who have kids with special needs that simply don't get talked about. Professionals ask us to share so many details. This exchange of information is a necessary evil if our children are to get the help they need. At the same time, though, it's a massive invasion of privacy. Some aspects of our lives can't be shared with just anyone.

I have the advantage of being in a safe place as I write this. I've experienced the things I'm writing about, and I have the advantage of hindsight to help me understand exactly what happened. I can take a break from my writing at any point. If something I'm writing makes me sad or angry, I can take the time to regroup and calm down before I finish what I'm trying to say. We don't have that luxury going into new situations. There is usually only so much time to receive, process, and respond to information. Perhaps you will be able to see yourself in some of the situations I write about, and maybe you'll realize that you're not alone and that you're not the only one to have something awkward or seemingly cruel happen to you.

I worked for many years in various positions funded through grants from the federal or state budgets. During those years, it was part of my job to help families work with the agencies that served their children. The underlying premise is that children are best served when families and agencies work together. It makes sense, and it actually does work thusly in many cases. The problem is that people work in these agencies, and budgets, funding, personal agendas, and prejudices get in the way. The result becomes something less than what was intended. I will elaborate on this theory of mine throughout this book.

I've long felt that there should be some type of record of my life since my children arrived on the scene over twenty-five years ago. Throughout the very early years of their lives, I wrote about my experiences. At first, I wrote as a means of therapy because I had no one I could talk to. All of our friends with families had typical kids, without all the medical and behavior issues our kids had. My husband isn't the type of person you can talk to about feelings, and that's what I needed. So I wrote instead.

At first, it was just for me. Writing those short stories gave me the outlet I needed. I then developed a newsletter for the early intervention organization I was working for. I would insert one of my stories in each issue, and they were very well received. As a result, I created a site online where I published most of my stories. It has been accessed by many people over the years, and I've gotten many supportive comments. Several universities have requested permission to use some of my stories in their classes for special education teachers. The site no longer exists, but you can see much of the content it had at http://patlinkhorn.org.

Much of what you will see in this book was included online. Over the years, I've toyed with the idea of putting these stories together in a book. The site was the basic version of my story. This is the gold premium version. Plus, I am no longer working for any organization, so I don't have to watch what I say. This is a brutally honest story.

So, the time is here, the time is now, and I'm going to give it a shot. If it helps only one person, it will be worth the effort.

I may have thought my life had its bad points before the arrival of my children, but my two inspirations have taken me on journeys to the depths of despair, as well as to some of the most joyous, wonderful places a person could go.

I know that sounds a bit sappy, and I am not one of those devoutly religious people who has a message to share. I'm just an ordinary person who was dealt a raw deal, and I had some pretty tough decisions to make if I was going to have any kind of life at all.

Humor saved me and continues to save me. You have to realize that you are only one in billions of people. In the big picture, who really gives a hoot? I read something a while back that I'd like to share with you.

> If you are kind, people may accuse you of selfish, ulterior motives; be kind anyway.
>
> If you are successful, you will win some false friends and true enemies; succeed anyway.
>
> If you are honest and frank, people may cheat you; be honest and frank anyway.
>
> If you find serenity and happiness, they may be jealous; be happy anyway.
>
> The good you do today, people will often forget tomorrow; do good anyway.
>
> You see, in the final analysis, it is between you and God; it was never between you and them anyway.
>
> —Mother Teresa

God and I have an ongoing dialogue. I may not have a designated time to pray each day, but I often gaze skyward and ask, "What do you have for me today?" or "What the hell are you thinking? There's no way I can deal with this!" Sometimes I do what I want to do, and sometimes I do what I think God would want me to do. Most of the time, I just go into forward mode and do what I feel I need to do.

We have to do what feels right and what our gut tells us to do. Sometimes I've had no reason other than that it sure seemed like the right thing to do at the time. Sure, I've made mistakes, but they've been my mistakes. But they've come from who I am and with no intent to do harm.

I also feel there needs to be something written about how parents advocate for their kids. When you hear parents of kids with disabilities say that their children are blessings, it's not an idle remark. They truly teach us lessons we would never have learned otherwise. They teach us all about things like humility and what things in life are important. They remind us that we are pitifully human and not able to be in control of our lives. They teach us to rise above the pettiness of the world and that we can accomplish feats we never would have thought possible.

But enough of that! This book isn't just about all that stuff. It's also about survival. It's about finding the humor amid the absurdity of our lives. True, there are times in the lives of parents who have children with exceptional needs when tears are the only possible outlet for our emotions. After the tears, as I've read countless times, (so it must be true) comes the grieving process.

I believe in grief. It does happen. But it's so much more than that! Grief may be the trigger for all those other emotions like anger and denial. I don't think that all of our anger and denial stem from our children's disabilities. Much of it comes from the reactions of society to us and our children. Maybe we wouldn't notice it so much, except that from our view of the situation, we see things in a different light. Our view of life comes from where we're sitting in the bleachers. I don't think that we parents have tunnel vision and can see things only from our viewpoint. I think we see way too much, and that's why the absurdity of all the other people becomes so apparent.

My children can—and have—compensated for and (in some cases) overcome aspects of their disabilities. They're not the bad guys here. They're the heroes. People put up needless barriers for our children to overcome, in addition to those their bodies and minds have imposed on them. Were these people not so stupid, there would be no absurdity. Maybe *stupid* is a rather crude word—uninformed or biased might be better. But I'm getting off track. This book is meant to be what I call a good bathroom book: You can pick it up, read a random chapter, and put it down until next time. Hopefully, after reading a chapter, you'll go away with a bit more understanding about a situation you might have encountered in your own life. I hope that you might perhaps even begin to be able to see the humor in life. If you happen to shed a few tears, just remember that if eyes are the windows to our souls, tears are what make the windows clean.

Chapter One

Off the Fence at Last

I spent close to twenty years working within the disability and special educational system. I have children with disabilities, and I actively advocated for better services for them. I also worked with and for professionals and agencies that provided services to families and their children with disabilities and developmental delays. I could never be completely parent or completely advocate or mentor. I had to balance the needs and requirements of both roles, so I felt as if I had one foot on each side of the proverbial fence.

In theory, I should have been able to develop a baseline of how I could or should react to different situations. Yes, there were guidelines, and yes, I was a mentor to parents and not the voice of the parents. I was there to explain the rights to the parents and to help them work with the system. On paper, that is pretty straightforward. In reality, this was not so much so.

At one point, I worked with six different school districts. Each had its own personality. To further complicate things, each building within each school district—preschools, elementary schools, middle schools, and high schools—had its own personality, as well. The principal of each school had his or her own views and policies for his or her building. In addition, the special education coordinators for each district had the authority to approve or commit the school district to provide specific services. The principals and special education coordinators were those about whom I needed to know the most.

We can't forget the teachers. They were the hands-on people who actually spent the most time with the children. They could make a plan work, or they could make it fail. Over the years, I've met some wonderful special education teachers and some awesome regular education teachers. I've also met some in both categories who were probably better suited to ditch digging.

I've also had many, many off-the-record conversations with teachers and aides who would call me off to the side and say, "You can't say you heard this from me, but this is what's really going on."

When my kids were in grade school and in classes with their regular-education peers, I always asked that the teacher who volunteered to have them in their class be their teacher. When I passed this strategy on to other parents, it sometimes worked for them. Sometimes, though, it didn't because some schools have practices or policies that don't allow for that type of choice.

Some school districts liked me. Others hated me. Some parents actively worked to learn what their rights were, and others just wanted me to fix the problems. Each situation called for different approaches. Much of what I was able to do depended on my relationship with the professionals involved.

One special education coordinator was known to say no before you could finish the question. Another went out of his way to provide the best services available.

One strategy I used with a lot of success was to ask parents if I could call the school so I would know exactly what kind of services their children were currently receiving. It also gave me a chance to talk to the teacher or principal and get those people's perspective on what was happening. It further served to let the school know that I was involved in helping the parent and was interested in both sides of the story.

Many times, that one call could resolve a problem. Parents hear what is being said but don't always understand what is meant. Schools sometimes use jargon with which parents aren't familiar. Oftentimes, emotions are running so high that words have no meaning for parents. There were many cases in which both parties were saying the same thing but were using different words.

One agency I worked for was aghast at this strategy and told me I was never, under any circumstances, to ever call the school. I'm still shaking my head over that one!

I also worked under different conditions with different agencies. One agency did spot-on evaluations on my job performance. One said, "Here, fill this out. Don't make it too good." Others filled out evaluations even if they had had no contact with me over the past year. Another did yearly evaluations, but when I asked for clarifications on some comments, my request was ignored and my contract wasn't renewed. Go figure!

It's the same with all agencies and school districts. Policies don't matter if they aren't implemented. People and their personalities play a big part in how things happen. A misinterpretation of what was said can set the tone for an entire meeting. Limitations in what you can say can make a difference. Interpretations of rules or policies can vastly affect outcomes.

One time, a friend whose wife taught in one of my school districts told me what his wife told him had been said at a staff meeting. (Are you totally confused yet?) The staff had been told to not tell parents that their children were having difficulty seeing things written on the chalkboard or that they appeared to have difficulty seeing the words in books because said parent might demand that the school pay for eyeglasses. My job prohibited me from saying anything about it.

I could go on and on. After twenty years, I can say I've pretty much seen it all. Needless to say, once I was unemployed, the first thought that came to mind was that I didn't ever have to be nice to nasty professionals or overly demanding parents again. I could finally get off the fence.

And now you know the rest of the story. Wait, that was Paul Harvey's line, and it came at the end of the story, not in the first chapter. The real rest of the story is that I'm now able to share my experiences and thoughts with no restrictions. The articles I've written over the years are all through this book. They are not in chronological order, and they are not all about my kids. Some were written for a general audience. It's about experiences we may share. You may not always agree with me, and that's okay. We are all different, and our experiences define who we are. Just keep an open mind.

Chapter Two

You Get What You Got

S ometimes life doesn't always give you what you want. Sometimes life gives you exactly what you didn't want. That's the way it seemed to me. You will see some basic statistics on my two girls below.

Kimberly Sue, born: June 18, 1985
Birth weight: Three pounds

She was in foster care from birth until November 1986. When we adopted Kim at sixteen and a half months, she didn't walk, talk, or hold her own bottle. My husband and I had tried to have a child of our own for many years and finally decided to adopt. Kim was the first child we actually saw, and it was love at first sight. She progressed a great deal after she came to live with us, but it was soon evident that she was a wild child with some pretty severe behaviors. She threw tantrums, ate glass, destroyed everything of sentimental value I owned, refused to be potty trained, and ran off every chance she got.

Kimberly received early intervention services (services for children birth to three years of age with developmental delays or disabilities) until she was three years old. She attended preschool at the local board of developmental disabilities in our county until she was five

5

and a half years old. We then moved her to the local school district, where she was in kindergarten for a year and a half. Kim's first grade year was spent in a self-contained classroom. When she began second grade, inclusion was the thing, and she was one of the first children with delays to be part of a regular class. This has continued over the years, with all involved learning how to best serve her.

Over the years, Kim has had several diagnoses: attention deficit disorder, attention deficit disorder with hyperactivity, mental retardation, and finally autism. It wasn't until we received the diagnosis of autism that we were truly able to help Kim.

Today, she is a fairly successful young lady of twenty-eight with a much better future than any of us could have imagined all those years ago.

It's only been in the past few years, after connecting with two of Kim's biological siblings, that we found out her biological mother had a type of schizophrenia and also used crack cocaine. Kim may actually be a fetal alcohol kid, but we've always treated her and have gotten services based on the autism diagnosis. That changes her diagnosis in one sense but really doesn't affect any treatment or intervention.

Krystal Leighann, born: June 18, 1987
Birth weight: One pound, two ounces

Krystal was conceived soon after we adopted Kimberly. She didn't want to miss Kim's second birthday, so she was born about three months early on Kimberly's birthday. She spent the first six months of her life in Children's Hospital in Columbus, Ohio. Krystal had to have a patent ductus operation to close a valve that normally closes in full-term pregnancies, a ventricular shunt to keep fluid from accumulating in her head, cryotherapy to try to halt the progress of her retinas detaching, and a cricoid split to enlarge her airway (it was constricted due to the accumulation of scar tissue in her airway caused by the ventilator that had kept her alive). She finally came home in December 1987 with an apnea monitor, oxygen, and assorted medicines. She was also blind. As if all this weren't enough for one little girl, she developed a seizure disorder right after she turned three. Krystal also received early intervention services and preschool services for children with disabilities. She attended kindergarten three days a week at a special school for visually impaired children about twenty-five miles from us. She attended her home school on the other two days. When she started first grade, it was at her home school. She stayed there through the sixth grade. At that point, it was her decision to transfer to the Ohio State School for the Blind.

Krystal is now twenty-six years old. She has taken ballet and gymnastics, was the treasurer of her 4-H club, has won several art awards, has many trophies from showing her llama, and is a very bright young lady. There are also several areas she has problems with, but we manage.

Chapter Three

In the Beginning

In the beginning of my journey, I was a mess. I didn't look like it because I'm a firm believer in the Gerry and the Pacemakers philosophy of never letting the sun catch you crying. If you know what I'm talking about, then you're getting awfully close to being older than dirt. If you are clueless as to who this Gerry might be, he's a member of an old English band, and the song is one you might want to listen to.

When Krystal was born, no one was prepared. My water broke, and we were off to the hospital. I was only twenty-three and a half weeks along. I had no idea what was happening. They put me in a back room on the maternity ward and wrapped a monitor around my belly. They told me my water had broken, but that sometimes it seals back up. In the meantime, I was to just lie quietly. Something was mentioned about giving me an injection that would help the baby's lungs develop, but someone said I wasn't far enough along for it to help because the baby would never survive.

I was there for what seemed like hours. Every so often, a nurse would poke her head in and look at the readings on the machine and leave. My back was killing me. It was dark, and I was alone, so I cried.

Finally, an older nurse came in, asked how I was doing, read the machine monitor, and did some poking around. "Why, honey, you're in labor! The baby is just too small to register on the monitor."

Then things began to happen! They wheeled me into the delivery room, called my doctor (who happened to be on vacation), and waited for the OB/GYN on call to come. Krystal came before him, and the nurse said, "Oh my God! She's breathing!" And things got even more hectic.

Enter Dr. John Schowinsky. My hero! He was able to intubate her, and they whisked her away. I could continue with this story, but at this point, I'm going to insert the very first story I ever wrote.

Who Am I? Where Am I?

Where am I? What are all these tubes for? Who are all these people? The machines! Am I someplace in the future? Is this what happens when you eat anchovy pizza before bed?

Wait. I remember. Oh my God! Where's my baby? Wait, here comes someone. Hey, lady! Can you tell me what's going on? Is this a dream? No, not a shot. I need some answers!

Later

Wow! What a terrible dream! I'm in a strange place, and there were all these machines and tubes. I'm almost afraid to open my eyes. What if I'm still there? Hey, it must not have been a dream because all that stuff is still here. Maybe I've turned into Alice, and I'm in Wonderland. More like Horrorland, if you ask me. But I'm beginning to remember. I thought the baby had given my kidneys a real healthy kick, but they told me it was my water breaking. But I just started my Lamaze classes, so that can't be.

They put me in that back room. My back was killing me. They had that belt thingamajig around my stomach. Wasn't it supposed to tell them I was in labor? Good thing that older nurse came back and was able to tell them I really was in labor. Who knows what would have happened. But wait. What did happen? *The delivery room.* I remember now. But where's the baby? I saw her. She was moving. Where did they take her?

Oh good. Here comes my husband. He'll tell me what happened. Wait. What's that he's saying? Just over a pound? They're coming to get her? *Who's coming to get her?* I want to see her! Leave me alone. I don't like what you're saying. My baby will live. She has to! What? I'll get to see her before they come? Can I hold her? No!? Oh, she has to stay in the, what was it you called it? The incubator. Yes, that's it. Well, okay, if she has to. Here they come with her now. Dear Lord, I've seen newborn puppies bigger than her. What are all those tubes and wires for? She looks so uncomfortable. Don't all those things hurt her?

Okay. I know they're here to take her. Can I go too? Tomorrow? But I want to go with her now! So what if I leave anyway? That's my baby! Oh, all right. I'll go back to bed, but I will leave tomorrow. You have *my* word on that. At least leave that picture with me.

Please, Mom, Dad, Gary, go home. I'm tired. I want to sleep. No, I'll be okay. Please, just leave. Yes, I want to talk to a doctor. I need some answers.

What's he saying? Intubated? What? The next forty-eight hours are what? Oh, crucial. Yes, I understand that word. Does she stand a chance, Doctor? Is she suffering? Oh, they don't feel pain. (Does he think I'm an idiot?) She can't cry? Oh, because of the oxygen tube. Yes, I understand. She looked like she was crying, though. Twenty percent chance. Yes, I understand percentages. But it gets better with each hour? She did breathe on her own for a while, though, didn't she? Yes, I understand that her lungs aren't completely developed yet. Hey, I'll pray, okay? Thanks for answering my questions, Doctor. Yes, I'll be okay. Tired now.

Dear God, please, please, please. I'm begging you. Don't let her die. Please let her live.

Next Day

She's still alive? Hey, I knew she could do it. Why, you should have felt how hard she could kick! What? No, I don't want a shot to dry up my milk. Yes, I'm sure. Hey, lady, I'm sure, so leave with that needle. I want to go see my baby. What? A name? We hadn't decided on one yet. Wait, let me call my husband. He doesn't care, so I'll call her Krystal. Krystal Leighann. No, it's L-e-i-g-h-a-n-n. Yes, I'm sure. I don't care how other people spell it. And Krystal is spelled with a K and an a-l. No, I don't want that shot!

Later, Driving to the Hospital

What? I don't want to talk about where we'll bury her because she's *not* going to die! Okay, have it your way. Make your plans, but don't count on me and Krystal being there for the funeral, because that little girl is going to live. I'm not upset. Don't worry. I'll be all right. Is that all the faster you can drive?

At the NICU

God, my hands are shaking. She's in that room? Sure, I'll wash my hands and put that gown on. Time to go in. Calm down, walk slowly. What a horrible place! I'm in a time warp. This can't be happening to me. Where is she? Way back in that corner? Breathe, breathe deeply. Stay calm. All the other babies look so much bigger! She doesn't even have enough meat on her for there to be a crack in her little butt. It's perfectly flat. God, please help this little girl. She's made it this long. Please help her. Please.

What? Apnea? Levels? Monitor? Why can't I understand these people? Why won't they look at me? If I just don't cry and try to look like I'm in control, maybe they'll tell me more. I wish my hands would stop shaking. I wish I could wake up. This really can't be happening to me. I know, if I see the white rabbit, I'll know it's a dream. Just white uniforms. No white rabbit. It must be real. How am I supposed to act? Did they teach us this in school? Maybe they did, and I just can't remember.

How can these young kids be doctors? Why are they so rude? Why won't they give me straight answers? Hey, it's worked so far, acting like I'm in control. But don't they know I *need* to cry? Don't they realize I can't keep this all inside? But if I do, they'll make me leave and I want to stay with my baby. She's so tiny and helpless. Look, she's grown a silly millimeter! Hold on there. Laughing is as dangerous as crying. They'll think I've lost it.

What is the proper protocol here? Can anyone tell me how I should act? Can anyone understand? These doctors act as if I'm invisible. Please, just explain what that means. Just once. I'll go home and look it up, and I'll never ask again. Just please, tell me in English. She's *my* baby!

Here comes that nice vent person. I'll be able to find out more from him than all these other people put together. He acts as if I have a brain.

Everyone acts as if I'm made of glass and will break any moment. Don't they know I shattered a long time ago and I'm still functioning? Trying to always be in control only makes it harder, but everyone shies away from the slightest indication of tears. Can anyone understand? I want to wake up. I don't want to be here, and my name isn't Alice.

Chapter Four

Coping

We spent about six months at Children's Hospital in Columbus, Ohio. Krystal had several surgeries while she was there. They closed the patent ductus almost as soon as she got there. Poor little thing had so many parts of her that weren't quite done cooking, so they hooked her up to machines, operated on her, supplemented her intake, treated for and against different things, and poked her mercilessly.

Here is a picture of Krystal a day or so after she arrived at Children's Hospital. She had lost about half an ounce, but she was still alive. As you can see, she's hooked up to lots of gadgets. It was hard to look at her and not feel your heart breaking. We just stood around her incubator and looked at her. We couldn't hold her and could barely touch her through the hole in the unit. I spent many an hour up there in some sort of fugue state, staring at bits and pieces of her because looking at her as a whole was just too hard to bear.

The nurses there were awesome. I couldn't visit her daily because we lived seventy-five miles away and we still had Kimberly at home. We'd had her for only about seven months, and she was just beginning to bond with us so I alternated days between the girls. I'd call the hospital on the days I couldn't visit, and the nurses would update me on how her night had been, which doctors had been in to see her, and how much weight she had gained. I kept a tablet with me, and each day, I'd write down how much weight she had gained. Those ounces slowly crept up!

Someone suggested that we get her a small stuffed animal so we could compare the two of them and actually see how much she was growing. We bought Mr. Froggy. If you look closely, you can see that Mr. Froggy is about eight inches tall. He was with Krystal the entire time she was in the hospital. We actually bought two of him, so we could show people who couldn't come to see her exactly how small she was.

Think of a pound of hamburger. She weighed that much when she was born! She was only twelve inches long. Take that hamburger, and stretch it out until it's a foot long. Not much mass there! The frog was actually quite a bit wider than she was!

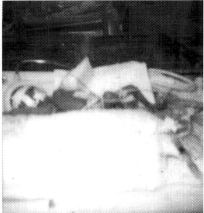

That was only the beginning. My husband and I coped in different ways. He felt it was his job to continue to work every day because of the staggering medical bills. He assumed that I would do the motherly

thing and be responsible where the children were concerned. They say the stress of something like this can destroy marriages, and I can understand why. I'm not going to tell you that we didn't have problems, because we did. I was fortunate enough to still have my own parents, and they were the people to whom I really opened up. They kept me sane because they were so optimistic. My in-laws are more conservative people when it comes to displaying their emotions, and I came to understand that my husband didn't fall too far from the tree. I truly believe my husband, Gary, has some very deep emotions but that he has a harder time displaying them, so he tends to distance himself. It's just the way some people are.

Chapter Five

How the Toilet Paper Rolls

For years, I've inwardly cringed every time I'd go into one of our bathrooms and see a new roll of toilet paper on the holder with the toilet paper put on in a such a way that you would have to push backward on the roll to get the paper to advance. In my mind, it's so much easier to have it roll forward. No reaching under and fumbling to find the end. You don't have to touch the wall (and when your kids are small, you get lots of fingerprints on the wall using that method) to actually be able to get a grip on it. The forward method makes so much more sense to me. Just reach out and flick your fingers toward you.

My husband would invariably put the roll on backward. Being the tolerant person that I am, I would glare at the roll of toilet paper, mumble a few choice words, and change it to my sensible way. It was not an issue that needed to be on my issues-that-*must*-be-addressed list. It could go on my issues-that-can-be-overlooked-because-they're-not-that-important list. But it was a sore spot. I just knew it was his way of annoying me without seeming to—his victory and my cross to bear.

This went on for years. Recently, Krystal went in to use the bathroom, and when she came out, she told me the toilet paper had been on backward and that she'd fixed it. Now pay attention to this dialogue, and you'll learn a very valuable lesson.

> Krystal: "Mom, the toilet paper was on backward. I fixed it."
> Me: "Oh, your dad must have put it on. He always puts it on backward."
> Dad, piping in from the living room: "I didn't know there was a right way to put it on."
> Me: "Oh yes, there is a right way," and I went on to explain my toilet paper theory.

My aha moment! He didn't know there was a right way! All those years, all that gritting of the teeth, and those tolerance points I'd been awarding myself—for nothing. He simply didn't know. I'd explained it to the girls when I taught them how to put a new roll on. I hadn't explained it to him because he was an adult, and I just figured his mother had taken care of that aspect of his training. Wrong!

Now take this very important life lesson, and apply it to other instances in your life. There's a surprising amount of stuff people don't know. When you're dealing with unique children, there's a list three hundred miles long of things you've learned and now know that all those other people never had to learn. Many times, people simply don't know. You have to be smart enough to know when they're ignorant of certain facts and when they're just too stupid to know any better. That can be a tough call at times.

Let me give you a few examples.

There once was a judge at a llama show who decided to give Krystal, who is visibly (no pun intended) blind, and another boy, who was visibly afflicted with cerebral palsy, special ribbons for the llama class they participated in. My other daughter, Kimberly, who looks and can act like a typical person, didn't get a ribbon. I immediately jumped into mom/advocate mode, and there were some harsh words exchanged. She thought she was doing a wonderful thing. I thought she was singling them out and discounting them as real people. It turned into quite an ordeal.

But the fact is that she didn't know how I felt about them being treated as real, normal people. We had paid the real, normal fees to enter the class. We hadn't asked for special ribbons. We had worked very hard to get where we were, and a special ribbon pretty much told us it didn't matter. We were discounted because we were different.

There were many people that day who helped implement that decision and a few others who thought it was a great idea. I found out that day that many of the people who I thought were accepting of our goals for our daughters actually weren't. They subscribed to the theory that special people need special treatment. There is a difference in special treatment and accommodations. Accommodations put our kids on a level that is more evenly balanced.

Before I offend everyone who likes special awards, let me say that it's a matter of personal preference. I don't always pass up special treatment for my girls. And the concessions I make vary with each girl because they have different disabilities. They are individuals, and for me, that is the key. Just as all typical people have differences, so do people with disabilities. I can read fast and write fairly well. I struggle with numbers. My husband reads slowly, but has a much better grasp of mathematics. We're both considered typical, but we have different strengths. So it is with people with disabilities. You can't just lump them all in a disabled category and treat them all equally because they're not equal in their abilities or disabilities. We have to treat them as individuals.

> Everybody is a genius. But if you judge a fish by its ability to climb a tree, it will live its whole life believing that it is stupid.
> —Albert Einstein

Chapter Six

Who We Are

Understanding is much deeper than knowledge. There are many people who know us, but very few who understand us.
—Author unknown

I'm always finding inspiration in the many quotes I see on my Facebook page. This one pretty much slapped me on the face this morning. It's the perfect introduction to a topic I think needs to be explored.

Parents of children who have disabilities are not all the same. We are as diverse as any other group. We come from different backgrounds and have different expectations, different home situations, different views of the world, and a whole host of other differences. We probably have more bad hair days than most people because our kids' needs usually come first.

Much as people classify our kids, they tend to do the same with us. But we see things from where we're sitting in the bleachers. When we're new to all this, we're down there sitting in the first row, and we can only see what's there on the bottom. We can look up and see the sky, but we can't see what's beyond. As we progress and learn more, we get to move up in the stands. Our view becomes wider, and we're able to see more. Our understanding grows. Our perspective may change. We may move up a few rows and not like what we see, so we move back down to safer territory. At any given time, there will be parents sitting in all the rows, but never all on the same row.

Sometimes we get stuck on a row, and we can't move up because we've run into a situation that makes it impossible to move on. Such might be the case when one parent accepts the disability and the other refuses to. An example might be the mother who knows the child has a problem, such as ADHD, and the father refuses to acknowledge that there is a problem. Poor Mom knows the child needs help, but Dad refuses to cooperate, and the child suffers. It's like trying to get past the fat man with a cooler in your row.

What can you do? Sit there forever or figure out how to get past him? Many parents find themselves in these types of situations. The fat man may represent a spouse or other family member. He may represent a belief you have that doesn't exactly jive with what you need to do. You can try to be nice and ask him politely to let you pass, or you may have to call security to make him move. Sometimes it's a leap of faith as to what you need to do because the results you seek may not be a given. They may just be a dream that requires you take the next step.

I once met a mother of a child with a disability who thought it was very important to always have her daughter dressed to a tee. This mom told me that it was important that her daughter always look her best because she was different and people would notice more if she wasn't dressed just so. I personally think that this was one way for this mom to cope. It was something she could control, and control is one of the things we lose when we have a different kind of kid.

Pat Linkhorn

To some people, how they dress is very important. I've always been more a comfort dresser than a trendsetter. If it feels good and happens to look good, I'm happy. If it doesn't look so good, but the comfort factor is way up there, I'm still pretty happy. I wear my favorite clothes out and have a wake for them when they finally get to the point where they're too shabby to wear anymore. At the time I met this mom, Kim was still undressing herself whenever she could get away with it, and Krystal still needed clothes that would accommodate her various tubes and gadgets. Fashionable clothing wasn't at the top of our list!

Some parents want to talk endlessly about their kids. It's their therapy to talk about them, and that's okay. We all need to deal with things in the way most comfortable for us. Others don't want to talk about their kids too much because it makes them uncomfortable to share those things that aren't working out. Those parents may become reclusive and not go out much.

I tended to not want to go out much, but at the same time, I didn't want to give up doing some of the things I'd always done, such as going out to eat. So I took my kids to restaurants, but tried to shield them from the views of others. I'd just glare at the people who stared at us. As I grew more comfortable being in public, Krystal got older and became quite the Chatty Cathy. She always wanted to engage in conversation with the people in the adjoining booth. She has always been quite open about her visual impairment, and she enjoys explaining to people that she is blind and that blind people read Braille and use canes. I've also become more open to explaining to people about the girls. We all change the way we react to certain things over time as we become accustomed to the way our lives have changed. It all goes back to where we are sitting in those bleachers at different times in our lives.

It can also be such a hassle to get all the necessary equipment loaded that it's just easier to stay home. With the high cost of gasoline these days, sometimes we have to stay home more than we would like to. The Internet and telephone still give us that connection to the outside world, so we're not really that alone. Parents can get all kinds of answers by calling various organizations. Some parents know what they want to hear. The following is a short story about just that.

Take a tip from your kids: Ask until you get the right answer

Kids have the right attitude. If they ask mom for permission to do something and she says no, they go directly to dad and ask the same question. Sometimes it works, and they get a yes from dad. Sometimes not. But they know what they want to hear, and the no answers aren't acceptable, so they keep asking.

Parents who have children with developmental delays and disabilities get questions. Lots of questions. Many times, when a question arises, it's not really a question. It's a confirmation. In other words, people know what they want to do. They simply want someone to confirm that what they want is valid or reasonable.

Truly stubborn parents will ask this question of every professional they come in contact with until they get the assurance they're seeking. The new or timid parent will accept the negative answer and go no further. The point here is not to imply that professionals don't have the right answers. They do have the answers to what they think you have asked. They don't always have the answer you actually want to hear, though.

Also, every person is at a different space and time in the disability movement. The director of the county board program might give you a different answer from a teacher who teaches in an inclusive setting or the speech pathologist who teaches in more than one program. None of them will give you the wrong answers, but each will answer from his or her own perspective. If you are not satisfied with the answer you get, or if you feel someone really didn't understand the question, don't stop asking. Ask the next parent or professional you encounter.

Parents are always at differing points in the disability movement, so they too might give you different answers to the same question. You have the option of asking this question as many times as you want, though. You may have twenty-five different answers, and when you ask the twenty-sixth person, you may finally get the answer you've been seeking. When you get that answer, you'll know it. Suddenly, what you should do will seem clear, and there will be no more doubt as to the course you should take. The question will have turned into a fact that requires action.

Here's an example of this type of question. A parent asks, "I have a five-year-old kid with a specific disability. My two-year-old child is displaying many of the same symptoms. My older child got a lot more services once he had his diagnosis. Should I get a diagnosis for the younger one now or wait until she is three?"

This question was asked of a panel of experts. The parent got three different responses. One person responded that it took only one delay to receive early intervention services, another responded that she was probably more likely to recognize the problem since she'd had experience with her other child, and one told her that she should get her diagnosis now, so she could receive services from the school system when her child turned three. The final answer was probably the answer the parent was seeking. She just wanted some confirmation that what she wanted to do was right.

The three different answers she got to her question were all correct. Yes, her child qualified for services now. Yes, due to her previous experience, she probably was correct in her assumption, and yes, she should get a diagnosis now. The total of the answers gave her a more complete answer, but only when you have a group of professionals do you receive that kind of answer. Usually, it's a matter of asking the same question to different people at different times before they all add up to such a complete answer.

So as I stated at the beginning of this essay, ask until you get the right answer. The method you instinctively knew as a child was right.

What I tried to demonstrate in the previous short story is that sometimes it works to take this approach, although there will be times when there may not be any solution, so you work around the problem.

When I was working with parents, there would be times when a parent would call with a problem or concern. It would usually concern something the school had done. The solution or answer to the problem would involve talking to other people (who may not be available for several days) or researching an answer (which would take time depending on what else I had to do). Perhaps it wasn't something that I could help with. Parents would go on and on and tell me the same thing numerous times. I understood they needed an answer, but for a number of reasons, it simply wasn't possible to give them one at that time. Some of these parents would go down the list and call every agency they knew of. At the end of the day, they might still not have an answer, but they'd had a whole day of venting to many different people and might actually feel better even if there wasn't a good answer to their question.

The hardest aspect in working with parents is that 90 percent of dealings with them are crisis-oriented. I never seemed to get calls unless there was a problem. The best parents to deal with are those who are willing to learn exactly what their rights are. The worst kind of parents are those who want you to come in and fix the problem and never want to learn how to deal with it themselves in the future.

Throughout a child's life, a parent has to deal with various people. Some will be very helpful, some will be somewhat helpful, and others will downright difficult to deal with. They say one bad apple can spoil the whole bunch, and so it is with parents and professionals. A parent can go into a situation expecting the best and find they're confronted with a panel of educators who don't want to provide any type of service for a child. The parent may have quite a battle to even get a minimum of services. They go away with a different attitude, and when the next situation comes along, they go in expecting to have another battle.

Professionals never know what to expect from the parents they have to deal with, and it makes coming to an agreement difficult when one side is already primed to argue.

My advice is to go into any meeting with an open mind, but to be prepared for the worst in case it happens. It makes parents naturally defensive, but being prepared and knowing what the rules are ahead of time can make the process go better for everyone.

Bad things can happen even when people have good intentions. Let me tell you a story about Krystal when she was less than a year old. After she was finally discharged from Children's Hospital and got to come home, she developed pneumonia within a week and had to be hospitalized again. Scar tissue had formed in her airway, and they had to cut her throat, stretch her airway, and sew it all back together again. After the surgery, she had to be completely immobile for quite a while. We got a call in the middle of the night while she was up there saying things weren't looking too good. Needless to say, I was an emotional wreck. But, God was with us, and Krystal made it through.

Her stay in the hospital conflicted with an appointment we had scheduled with the retinal surgeon. I called to tell the doctor to cancel the appointment, and the doctor very casually replied, "That's okay. Her retinas are completely detached, and there's nothing I could do anyway."

Now, the eye department at the hospital had been saying she may have had a loss of some peripheral vision and would probably need corrective lenses, among some other somewhat hopeful things. When I stormed into the eye department's office at the hospital demanding to know why they hadn't told me the truth, they said they were sorry, but they didn't feel I would have been able to handle that information. I'm sure they thought they were doing what was right, but I don't think they thought beyond what would happen after I learned the truth. Maybe they thought I'd thank them for saving me the heartache, but in reality, I had to drive seventy-five miles home, alone in the pouring rain. I couldn't tell you whether it was the tears or the rain that made it so hard to see that night.

For quite a while after that, all the doctors I dealt with received the third degree about the information they were giving me. I'm sure many of them felt I was one of the most difficult parents they had ever had to deal with. The pain of my bad experience faded, though, and I eventually got back to being a somewhat likable person.

Chapter Seven

Agencies, Committees, Laws, People, and More

My dad used to tell me that all people put their pants on one leg at a time. He also used to tell me that all people weren't like us, especially when my choice of friends seemed dubious. So it took me awhile to figure some of this out.

Early on in my advocacy, I read a book by Rick Kirschner and Rick Brinkman called "Dealing with People You Can't Stand: How to Bring Out the Best in People at Their Worst." There are ten types of difficult people, and the book helped me to be able to instantly size up a situation so I could handle it better. The authors detail practical steps to take with each style of people, making it easier to increase your confidence in difficult situations. It is a must-read book. You will learn how to use advanced, sophisticated listening techniques to unlock the doors to people's minds, hearts, and deepest needs. The book tells you how to cultivate nine take-charge skills that turn conflict into cooperation by reducing the differences between people. It also explains how to change the destructive behavior of the tank: the know-it-all, the grenade, the whiner, and many more.

First of all, we'll talk about the laws. Don't panic! I won't be using long numbers referring you to obscure legal text. This is just my overview of how laws work.

Most bills are written with good intentions. The people who write them are probably really nice, and they have a vision of what a particular law will accomplish. They write the bill, they get it passed, and it goes out among the people to be implemented. So far, so good. But these lawmakers who are sitting behind desks most likely have no real experience with how this law will be interpreted by the people doing the actual work.

People tend to get hung up on what a word might actually mean. Good examples are the words *accommodation* and *modification*. What one person sees as an accommodation is actually perceived to be a modification by another person. Committees can get hung up on these types of things and spend endless meetings haggling over what is what. There are also some people who seem to make a career out of being on committees. I think it's mostly so they can debate issues with other people, have a nice lunch, and get away from the office for a day. The other thing about committees is that one person goes to the meeting and then goes back to work and doesn't inform the other people at work about what went on at the committee meeting, even if it might affect what everyone does at work.

I was once on a committee, and modifications and accommodations were an issue. We had three meetings debating wording in the intended committee report. I finally suggested that we first define exactly what those words meant before we wasted another meeting on it. Lots of people's balloons got busted that day because it meant they had to get on with the actual task of the committee, but it made sense to me.

Many committees require that a third of their members be parents of individuals with disabilities. Before you commit to endless meetings, make sure your input is actually wanted. Some federal funding requires the input of parents, and agencies are required to include us, but the professionals involved don't really want us to say anything or actually have an opinion. There are also parents of children with disabilities who work for agencies. They tend to get appointed to many committees to serve in the role of parents, but they belong to the agencies, and more often than not, they support that agency's policies. That's not to say they aren't committed to getting better services for their kids, but they are constrained by their jobs.

There was one year that I decided to end my involvement with several committees simply because I was one of their token parents. I was also employed by an agency, so my input was limited. I couldn't always say what I truly felt, or I might not have a job when I returned to the office. At the very least, I might be reprimanded and removed from the committee.

Another time, my daughter and I were on a special education subcommittee that required parent and client input. They never provided a Braille agenda for her. She and I were both token committee members. I found it so ironic that a special education committee wouldn't provide this accommodation for her. It seemed a committee like this one should set the standard for other committees. I was employed by an agency at this time, so I couldn't say anything that would reflect poorly on my employer.

Agencies are supposed to abide by the laws we talked about earlier. Most of the time, these agencies are run by people who believe in the policy of the agency. However, the same agencies require that a person who works for them must have a degree. Experience doesn't mean much. I am not saying that having a degree is a bad thing. On the whole, a degree is a useful thing to have. It means that a person had the initiative to attend college. The problem is that a degree provides you with the basics. It doesn't always provide you with the common sense you need to apply your skills to various situations.

Let's suppose you have a degree in social work. You've learned all the basics of being a social worker. Then you get a position working for an agency that deals with people with special needs. If it is an educational agency, there are laws for the people who require special education that protect them. You may never have had any dealings with anyone who had a disability. The laws are something you never had to learn about, and an agency usually doesn't provide you with a detailed training period to learn about these laws, so you jump right into the job and do the best you can. Many times, that's enough, but when a client has a concern that is beyond what you understand, it's the client who gets the raw end of that deal.

It may sound as if I'm out to bash all agencies and committees. It's not that at all. The truth is that my children wouldn't have received the services they did without agencies. I was lucky enough to have some truly caring people who did everything in their power to get appropriate services for my girls. They also valued what I could offer. I'm just telling you that agencies are imperfect. They are constrained by the rules that govern how agencies conduct their business. If they are funded through state or federal monies, there are guidelines they have to follow to continue to receive their funding from year to year. If it's a good agency, staffed by competent people, the people involved will refer you to someone who can actually help. At worst, the client will be told—and convinced—that their concern is invalid.

Another issue is budgets. Agencies can do only so much. Their manpower is limited to how many people they can employ. One legal agency I know of decides at the beginning of its fiscal year what types of issues they will handle. If an issue is a hot issue, the agency might have a certain number of cases it will handle. After that point, any additional people who might need help don't get it. It might also choose to not help with issues that have a low chance of being able to be resolved.

So what does this mean to the consumer? It means that the good intent of the law got caught up in agency policy and funding issues, and the consumer didn't get the protection or help the law was intended to provide.

There is also the issue of decreased funding to many agencies. People who work in these agencies often end up doing more than they were originally hired to do. One person's position may be cut due to decreased funding, but the services that person provided still need to be provided to the consumers. So the agency has to dole those responsibilities out to remaining staff. Throw in a few more cuts to staff, and pretty soon, people are required to do more and more. Their efficiency decreases because they have too many hats to wear.

Funding can also be an issue when it comes to one-on-one services. Employees of an agency may have their travel budget decreased. Rather than meeting with a consumer in person, they have to conduct their correspondence through e-mail or teleconferences. You lose so much that way. You can't read body language or facial expressions in a teleconference. E-mails tend to be cold and are often misinterpreted. It all adds up to a less-than-effective way to do business.

Agencies also tend to not always play well with each other. One may be funded through a federal law and another through a state law. They may collect their data in different ways, which can make sharing it difficult. Their criteria for providing services may also be different. It can make transitioning from an early intervention system into a preschool educational setting a nightmare for parents. Everyone tends to think that their way is the best way, and it's often difficult for the people who make the decisions to agree with others. Remember the list three hundred miles long of the things we've learned that others don't know? Well, agencies have their own long list of things they know about their agency that we don't know.

Sometimes it's about numbers. The number of individuals they serve may impact funding. Say that one staff person can serve ten people. If ten clients transfer to another agency, that might mean that one staff member needs to be let go. What is best for a client isn't always in the best interest of the agency. I know of one agency that files major unusual incident reports on another agency whenever it can. Its goal seems to be to eliminate that agency. Just forget that that one agency provides Internet and computer access to their consumers and the other doesn't. To me, since I am a techy type of person, that computer component is vital to independence for my girls. People who have access to computers and e-mail take it for granted. Where does it say that people with disabilities shouldn't have the same access?

Some of the best advice I ever got was when someone told me that people tend to regard their jobs as their kingdoms. A school principal may feel he is the king of that building, and you have to remember to treat him as such. You have to respect a person's right to rule his or her kingdom and realize that that person regards it that way.

You also have to realize that some kings can be dictators. A school principal once informed me that things were done "that way" in the bigger cities, but that they didn't do it that way there. We were discussing a very specific law in the IDEA (the federal Individuals with Disabilities Education Act) at the time. Another principal told me that he didn't believe kids had mental illnesses and that it was just a cop out to say they did. Yet another one told me that he'd been doing this for way longer than I had and that he knew a lot more influential people than I did.

This may all sound a bit depressing. It is, and it isn't. As a parent or consumer, you have to be knowledgeable about the laws and the way agencies operate. I was fortunate enough to be able to see both sides. Most of us don't have that advantage. Yes, it requires that the parent do more work. But you have to consider it an investment in your child's future. Remember, you are still going to be the parent and the one who knows the most about your child no matter what agency you are dealing with. Learn about the laws, and use that knowledge. Refer to it, and ask for written documentation on policies as well as written responses when you are told something can't be done. Keep a journal, file all papers, and document all phone calls. Don't be afraid to ask a person's superior about important issues. Sometimes, the people at the top don't know what the people below them are doing.

When my younger daughter was in grade school, I asked for her to have access to a teacher for the visually impaired. It was reported on the front page of a newspaper after a school board meeting that if a parent were to insist that the district follow federal guidelines for teaching visually impaired students, it could cost the district $190 every time the teacher was used.

The reasoning was that the hourly cost was fifty dollars. The school district would also have to pay for the two hours the teacher was traveling, plus forty dollars for mileage. The total was a whopping $190 each time that teacher spent an hour with my daughter. The board claimed the school had a teacher who knew Braille but was not certified. The truth was that the teacher was learning Braille as she taught my daughter. The teacher's intent was admirable, but think about it: Would you want any professional to provide a service for you that they were just learning? The article ended with, "The federal government requires that, but it doesn't provide any extra money to pay for it."

Was I upset? Yes, I was. There were so many things that were wrong with the whole thing. Since we live in a small community, everyone knew who the visually impaired student was. (There were two in our entire district at the time.) Everyone would think my child was the cause for any district hardship. It sounded as if we were literally taking candy out of the mouths of babies.

The first thing I thought was why they would have someone drive all that way to teach for only an hour. You'd get more bang for your buck if you had them stay two or three hours. We ended up finding a certified teacher for the visually impaired who lived only forty miles away. Once a week, she would come and spend an entire day at the school and leave assignments for an aide to implement. We probably still cost the school more money than it would have liked, but it wasn't nearly what it tried to make us believe it would be. Plus, the board seemed to feel that unfunded mandates were something that didn't apply to it.

My husband and I attended the next board meeting with copies of special education laws and anything else we could find to prove we knew what our rights were. The interesting thing about the whole ordeal was that I found out how totally uneducated board members were about special education laws and the rights of people with disabilities. If you think about it, most of their business deals with issues that pertain to the other 95 percent of the student population. After we spoke to the board, a lot of things were straightened out. Krystal got her Braille teacher, and the discussions about what my daughter needed were no longer front-page news.

The next confrontation we had with our local school district came about when Krystal began attending the school for the blind in a town about eighty miles away. The superintendent signed off on her attending that school. It cost the district nothing to send her there, but it was required to provide transportation.

Krystal wanted to be a residential student. She would spend the week there and come home on weekends. We decided that we would take her up each Sunday and have the school provide transportation home. The first few weeks we also picked her up and brought her home while the district was trying to figure out how to arrange transportation. The transportation director assured me that a plan for her transport was being working on. After about three weeks, I called the superintendent to find out what was going on. He informed me that there was another visually impaired unit in a school district closer to home, so our district wouldn't be providing any transportation. The superintendent had signed off on her attending the school for the blind, so I knew his reason wasn't valid. I called my husband, who called a board member he knew. In turn, the board member called someone and told that person that we were pretty well-informed parents, that we would file a complaint, and that the school district would probably lose. By the end of that day, transportation had miraculously been arranged.

If the call to the board member hadn't worked, I would have filed a complaint. In all likelihood, we would have won. My first step would have been to ask for that decision in writing. Schools will rarely put in writing anything they shouldn't be telling you. That's why it is so important to always ask for those things they refuse to give you be put in writing. Sometimes, that's all it takes, but not always. If they do put something in writing, you will have that to add to your complaint if you choose to file one.

Chapter Eight

Living with Autism

When Kimberly was still in school, her aide, Phyllis, was taking classes to become a social worker. The following is the result of one of Kimberly's aide's class assignments. She had a new question for me each week for twelve weeks. This was written while Kimberly was still in school.

How has having a child with autism changed your family dynamics?

It's been a long time since we experienced the dynamics of having no children. I'm not sure I even remember what it was like.

Gary and I had been married for nearly ten years before we adopted Kimberly. The five years before we got her were spent going through all the things you go through while trying to get pregnant. I had surgeries, took pills, and did anything the doctors suggested. Once we decided to adopt, we were faced with all the intrusions that go along with that. I'm not sure we had typical family dynamics that occur when you're childless by choice.

I'd been poked and prodded, and our personal life had been examined. What's typical about that?

Thinking back, though, Gary and I were able to do all the things we wanted to do. We had our home built, and I had my work and my horses. He had his work and his race car. We did things together, but we also pursued our own hobbies. I tended to do all sorts of crafts and projects and sort of went from one thing to another. He was the decision maker, and I was the wife. I was probably more aimless than he was.

I had a lot of independence, which I lost to a degree once we got Kim. I lost the rest of it when Krystal was born the following June. That's probably what I remember most about my life before kids. I had time to do what I wanted to, although probably not too much direction. I used to think I'd never run out of things to do because I was interested in so many things. I still do things for myself, but it's part of who I was before the kids came, and it's what keeps me sane.

How did having a child with autism change your life?

Once we adopted Kimberly, things changed. She required a good deal of supervision, but I was still able to work. I had a beauty shop in my home, so I was able to schedule my appointments around her schedule.

I believe I would have been able to deal with Kim and her problems and continue to work, but the birth of her sister changed all that and really impacted our family dynamics.

I became pregnant soon after we adopted Kim. Kim came home the middle of November. I got pregnant in January, and Krystal made a surprise entry into this world in June. She weighed just over a pound. Her first home was Children's Hospital in Columbus. She was there for six months. She finally came home with an apnea monitor, oxygen, and assorted medicines. She was also blind.

Kim progressed a great deal after she came to live at our home, but it was soon evident that she was a wild child with some pretty severe behaviors. She threw tantrums, ate glass, destroyed everything of sentimental value I owned, refused to be potty trained, and ran off every chance she got.

All of the issues with the children made it impossible for me to work, and that's where our family dynamics really changed. I had worked since I was eighteen. I was then thirty-five, and I had to rely on my husband's money. He was never stingy with it, nor did he ever question what I spent it on, but it was one of the most traumatic changes I had to make.

I'd lost my independence, in a sense. My life was consumed with these two children who seemed to consume all my time. Their problems seemed to grow by the day. I was overwhelmed and isolated. My world consisted of appointments with doctors and kids. The world I'd lived in before was gone. I had hoped that having kids would give me things in common with all our other friends who had kids, but we moved in an entirely different circle. They had typical kids, and we had kids with all these problems. There seemed to be no common ground.

Our life and marriage went through some pretty rocky times. Gary didn't realize how my life had changed. His had pretty much stayed the same. He went to work and associated with all the same people. His reasoning was that he had to work to make the money to support all our additional expenses. I went to most doctor appointments by myself. I didn't feel I had the support some other wives had. I'd go to the appointments and see husbands and wives there together. Looking back, I understand that since Gary is self-employed he didn't have the paid days off that some other people might have. Plus, I believe that when the kids were smaller, he didn't feel completely comfortable with them. He has gotten better as they've gotten older.

My saving grace was to become better informed. I researched everything and wrote hundreds of letters to find the answers I needed. Over time, I became the expert on the kids' problems, and Gary came to rely on my opinion. It was a way for me to have a degree of power and that seemed to replace the independence I'd lost.

When the kids got older, I was able to go to work for The Family Information Network, which was a birth-to-three program where I was able to share my experiences and help other families who had children with challenges. The hours were flexible, and it led to my present job as a parent mentor. Now I work with families who have kids in special education.

The major change in our family affected me the most. I entered a whole new world and pretty much left my old one behind. In most ways, Gary's life stayed the same. His only comment about this question was that he didn't have time to read the paper anymore, so that should support my theory! Things have changed for him, but I don't think it was as abrupt or dramatic as the way my life changed. Gary adhered to the way he was raised. The mom is responsible for the kids, and the dad works. He has come around and become more involved over time, but I am the decision maker for the kids and he accepts that. I don't mean to say that he doesn't have opinions or make decisions. He does, but I can see my influence on many of the ideas he has now. His life has changed gradually, and I don't think he realizes it as much.

Having a child with a disability can ruin a marriage or make it stronger. We went through some tough times, but looking back, I'd have to say that our experience has made us both better people.

What did you do?

We adopted Kim when she was sixteen and a half months old. She had been in foster care since birth. She had an older biological brother and sister who had been removed from the home prior to her birth. Kim weighed three pounds at birth, and from what we were able to find out, she was in the hospital about a month after her birth.

When we adopted her, we were told she had some problems, but my husband and I believed that with lots of love and attention, most of them could be overcome. Kim didn't walk, talk, or hold her own bottle when she came to live with us.

She learned to do all of these things in her first few months with us. She had been in adequate foster care. I believe they took care of her basic needs, but really didn't spend too much quality time with her. She hadn't had any early intervention, and she had had very few of the immunizations most children her age had received.

I enrolled her in our county's early intervention program, and she really made progress. All seemed to be going well. Kim had been so far behind due to her prematurity and the type of foster care she'd had, and I knew it would take awhile for her to catch up.

Very shortly after we adopted Kim, I became pregnant. Krystal was born very early and spent the first six months of her life at Children's Hospital in Columbus.

Poor Kim would spend a day at home with me, and the next day, she would be with her grandparents because I tried to visit Krystal every other day and we lived seventy-five miles from the hospital. The routine she had become accustomed to was changed, and as she got older, her behavior was changing. When we brought Krystal home, she was hooked up to oxygen and an apnea monitor and was basically confined to one room. Even with Krystal home, Kim still wasn't getting the amount of attention she needed.

She would have tantrums, eat glass and all sorts of other things, bang her head on the wall, run off, and more. We couldn't use the electric mixer or run the vacuum when she was awake. We took her to several different doctors and psychologists. They diagnosed her with developmental delays and ADHD.

I remember reading a book called "The Hyperactive Child" and finding that Kim behaved very similarly to the behaviors the book described. One doctor even put Kim on Ritalin. It may have helped, but I really can't remember. All I remember are the screaming fits and tantrums she would have when the medication wore off. We would have to physically hold her to subdue her when this happened. We soon came to the decision that we wouldn't medicate her until she began school and only then if it helped her learn.

I took parenting classes the county offered, and they saved my sanity. However, Kim wasn't getting any better.

When she was six, we took her to Western Psychiatric Hospital in Pittsburgh, Pennsylvania. They did a full-scale evaluation and diagnosed her with autism. I remember riding home that day and feeling devastated by the diagnosis, but at the same time, I was glad I finally knew what was wrong. The diagnosis fit Kim. I finally knew what was wrong, and it had a name. That was so much easier than dealing with the unknown.

What was the hardest thing to accept about the diagnosis?

The hardest thing about Kim's autism diagnosis was accepting that it wouldn't go away. When we first got the diagnosis, it was good to have a name for the way she acted. It also explained why she had some of the behaviors she had: the aversion to noise, always playing outside of a group of kids, her dislike of being touched, etc. It was overwhelming because there weren't very many other kids in the area who were autistic. The ones who were had some really bizarre behaviors.

Kim displayed many symptoms of autism, but we had been lucky. Since her sister was blind, we knew to do things repetitively and with a lot of tactile involvement. We also explained things to Krystal in a very detailed manner. These were some of the things they suggested you do for children with autism. Kim learned quite a bit that way, before we even knew what we should be doing for her.

What treatment was recommended?

When Kim was diagnosed with autism in Pittsburgh, the doctors suggested she attend a special school there. The distance from our home, about two and a half hours by car, was too great.

At the time, ABA (applied behavior analysis) was new. We looked into it, but the cost was enormous and living in a rural area has its drawbacks. Anyone who knew anything about it was at least sixty or seventy miles away. We didn't restructure our lives for Kim. With her sister and her problems, we had too much going on, so we did what we could.

I did lots of research, went to autism conferences, and talked to other parents. I was lucky enough to become involved with the Family

Information Network. I worked with parents from all over the state, so I had lots of resources.

Looking back, after seeing the way Kim learns, some intense ABA may have been very beneficial for her. I'll never know if it was a mistake not to pursue that.

What was the most trying experience while raising an infant with autism? Toddler? Adolescent?

On the whole, especially when Kim was younger, it was people's reactions to her. Many times, her behavior was inappropriate, and people would shy away from her or act visibly disgusted. If she had looked abnormal, it may have made a difference, but she looks so typical. I think many people just felt I wasn't a good parent.

How do you feel the schools handled a child with autism?

You're really opening up a can of worms by asking this question. If I would say it's been easy, I would be lying. It's been a battle from the beginning.

When Kim entered kindergarten, the principal was good. She didn't always agree with me, but we were always able to disagree and come to some sort of compromise. We were able to stop, step back, see the other person's point of view, and give it some credence. We both compromised on many occasions, and it worked. Of course, it helped that she seemed to honestly believe that all kids were worthwhile. She also wasn't locked into the belief that her way was the only way. She was able to change with the times. Inclusion began for Kim in her school.

I vividly remember one thing she told me. She said that teachers wanted parent involvement to be baking good cookies and helping their kids with homework, but not trying to become involved in their (the teacher's) teaching or how they ran their classrooms. After all, how dare parents even think that they could possibly have any idea how to teach children since they hadn't attended college specifically to learn how to do that? We are only the children's parents, and that is not where our expertise lies. (I'm not sure exactly where they think our expertise is.) It didn't take me long to realize that they would never give me everything I wanted. I also came to realize that all teachers aren't equal. Kim had some excellent special education teachers and some excellent regular education teachers. Unfortunately, she also had some pretty inept ones in both categories.

I came to understand that teachers see numbers and labels. The system forces them to. Unit funding, minimum and maximum class size, teacher qualification, and aides are just a few of the things they have to consider. Unless professionals have children of their own with disabilities, they can never really relate to what we see. These people haven't invested the time or the energy we have. Their futures aren't intertwined in the lives of these children. They have them for a few years, and their involvement in their lives is over.

Then add the fact that you have a multitude of different personalities. There are those people who believe different kids have just as much right to be in the regular classroom as typical kids. These are the teachers who do the best. They probably reach more of the kids in their class than the others. These teachers have seen Kim's potential. Some see only the deficiencies.

When Kim was in grade school, I actively fought for her to be included. When she had one of the good teachers, she did well. The years she had less-accepting teachers were horrible. She would lose everything she'd learned the year before because those teachers just let her be there and didn't try to include her or teach her anything.

The aides have ranged from downright bad to excellent. I'm not saying they were bad people—it's just that they weren't educated enough about autism. In fact, the whole system was pretty much uneducated about it. People may have gone to a conference or two, but no one in the district had the expertise to effectively teach her. Consistency was also lacking. It was a time when inclusion was the buzzword, and teachers were supposed to be working collaboratively. By that time, I was the parent mentor for several counties and saw the effects of that change in many different settings. If people were willing to change, it worked, but too many times, it came down to a territorial issue. In many people's minds, "those" kids still belonged in their own special room with their special education teachers.

By the time Kim entered middle school, I was getting tired. I was emotionally burned out. I had my vision for Kim to be a regular kid and be included with the regular kids, but it wasn't happening. In middle school, I was dealing with more teachers, and it was just too hard to try to make them all see the light. By that time, I'd realized that some of them never would.

They had a special education teacher and a special room there. Kim had some regular classes. I compromised and began to concentrate on the skills Kim would need in the real world. If they weren't going to be able to successfully include her, perhaps it was time to let go of my vision and get practical. It's a decision I made because I wasn't sure if I was reaching for my ideal or for what was best for Kim. I convinced myself that it was in Kim's best interest. I knew that having Kim in their classes had helped improve some teachers, but I also felt that it was my child who was the guinea pig, and when it didn't work, it was Kim who suffered. Looking back, I have to say that I regret it. I should have fought for more inclusion, but I took the easy way out.

I was afraid that high school would be our biggest challenge, but it turned out to be far better than I expected. The teachers at the high school were very supportive, and Kim was very successful there. Having Phyllis as her aide was great, but it has been a segregated environment. Kim had choir and FFA (Future Farmers of America) as regular classes. All the rest were with the other special education kids.

Much of Kim's education has dealt with social issues. She has made tremendous progress in that area. What she learns has to be applied to her real life. I'm not saying that her education has been bad. I think we all did the best we could. The teachers and aides did what they thought was right, and we all learned along the way. Their direction comes from administration. The teachers and aides really don't have much control over the way programs are administered. Have we done the best we possibly could? Probably not, and I blame myself for that. I wish I would have remained more focused on inclusive education. I've always said that Kim was not going to live in a segregated world. Hindsight is a wonderful thing. We learn from it.

Kim's class took regular trips out into the community. I always hated those trips because it was all the special education kids who went. Many of the things they did, such as going out to eat and shopping, are things I do with my kids all the time. The thing I hated about it was that Kim was going with all those other kids. I have a friend who works at the state hospital, and I often see her in Kmart with the residential patients from the hospital as they do their shopping. Kim's trips reminded me very much of that. I'm not sure we've made much progress in education when the two groups look so very similar.

I think the trips to the post office or to a place where the kids saw how things worked were helpful. That's learning.

Kim had 4-H judging the other day. She had to fill out a paper with her name and address and some information about her dog. She couldn't do it. She knew her name and the town she lived in. She can write her name, but not the rest of her address. That was something that has been on her IEP (Individualized Education Program) over the years.

Kim graduated with her class but went back to high school because they held her diploma. She had the right to be there until she was twenty-two. She had her evaluation with BVR (Bureau of Vocational Rehabilitation) for employment and although we hadn't had the official meeting, I got the impression that she was not ready for competitive employment. She wanted to work in the graveyard up the road, but she doesn't understand that the people have to want to employ you and that you have to fill out applications and apply for jobs.

I'm not sure that my compromises have worked. She has learned many things, but I'm not sure they have been the right things.

What do you think the school should do to better accommodate children with autism?

I think the schools need to be more informed about specific disabilities. They need to admit that they don't know things and look at kids as individuals rather than statistics. I think teaching to the content standards will go a long way toward more inclusive education for all special needs children.

How do you feel the public perceives children with autism? What could we do to change this?

The public perceives kids with disabilities as oddities. Look at all the programs there are for kids (such as Girl Scouts and 4-H). If there are accommodations that need to be made, they come from the individual group leaders, not the main organization. While it's true that most of the organizations allow adaptations, there usually are no written procedures. I think that speaks for itself.

What can we do? Well, we bring our kids out in the public eye and make people aware of them. Can we really change the way they feel? I'm not sure. I've had my kids involved in groups all their lives. The kids accept them, but very rarely are they fully included and embraced as equal members.

What was the best advice you received while raising your autistic child?

They're kids first. Expect for them the same things you would expect for a typical child.

What could you share with other parents of autistic children to help their family dynamics?

Your family isn't the disability. Keep it as normal as possible.

Do you feel your family dynamics have improved over time, or do you feel they have been challenged further?

Both improved and challenged. We have been forced as a family to learn more and to cope with more. It's never easy, but we're better for it.

Some parts of this questionnaire have been difficult for me to write. The questions about what the schools could do, what they could do better, and how society perceives children with autism brought up memories of things that have happened over the years.

It is my belief that my most consistent source of frustration hasn't been my children's disabilities or the way society perceives them. It has been the schools. Since I have two children with disabilities, it has been doubled. The very institution that is supposed to educate (and to know how to do so) my children has been the one that has put up the most barriers. They have questioned my parenting skills, our home life, and my children's right to be there. Luckily, the federal and state laws have supported me in all the supports I have asked for.

On the whole, the people in the system have been wonderful, but I'm afraid it's those who haven't been so great that made the more lasting impression.

Chapter Nine

For Professionals

Over the years, I wrote about my experiences for myself and special education newsletters. These ramblings of mine made their way to a website. The site was live for well over ten years, and during that time, many parents e-mailed me to thank me for sharing my experiences. Several college professors have e-mailed me to ask if they could use some of the things I wrote in their courses. It has been extremely flattering to hear from both groups. If you Google my name, you will find links to various other sites that have posted some of the things I've written. I'm sure that some people have used them without letting me know. I once found a piece I had written that someone else claimed as her own, which is another form of flattery, although I wasn't too happy about it. The company that hosted my domain went out of business, and I didn't have the foresight to download the content, so the original site is gone, but you can view much of that content at http://patlinkhorn.org.

The writings in this chapter have updates posted after each one since the text isn't always in disability-friendly language. That has been something that has evolved over the years. Many of the subjects are pertinent to parents and professionals alike, so I encourage you to read the sections for both parties.

Why Should You Listen to Me?

As parents, we are continually asked to make decisions. The decision could be about placement, discipline, or any number of things. Whatever the decision is, we have our own reasons for the decisions we make. The following story could be about any decision.

You may ask how I came to this decision. What qualifies me to say that I know better than you, a trained professional? Well, my life has taken a lot of twists and turns over the past few years. I've traveled roads that seemed to lead to nowhere, and I've had to take a lot of detours. I've actually visited places that you only dream about in your worst nightmares. But more important than the hard times I have had is the fact that I'm this child's parent. Whatever decision you make, it will have an impact on me. It will have a more beneficial impact if we can agree on the decision. But if we don't or can't agree, it may not be in the best interest of the child.

I know you may think my decision is an unwise one, but I didn't make it lightly. I lost many a night's sleep weighing the pros and cons. The problem seems to be that either way I go, I will have to make compromises and give up some things. I just happen to feel that the things I will have to give up if we do it my way are things that I can live more comfortably with.

Sure, I realize that you're a trained professional. I know you went to school specifically so you could do this. The books may have told you that your way is the right way. I didn't go to school to learn what I've learned. The need to learn it was just sort of there one day. Just say I took the crash course. You learned the easy way, by choice and with plenty of time.

Have you ever had to live with the results of the decisions you've made in your job? Have any of the decisions you've made affected your daily life? Have you ever considered that what the book said may be wrong in a given case?

This child will be living with this family long after you have moved on to another position or when we move on to the next program. The basis for continuing experiences with other professionals will be influenced during my experience with you. You can respect and value the impact I will have on this child and help me to build on the strengths that I have, or you can make me feel as if my concerns and ideas don't matter. You have the privilege of making it easier for me and for yourself and for your colleagues who will follow. I don't like the reasons we're here. If I had my way, I'd just as soon not be here with you. It would have been a whole lot easier if I had a child who didn't require your services, but it's not as if I have a choice. It is your decision whether to include me as a valued team member or to make me feel inadequate to do the job I have been given as this child's parent. So stop for a moment and think of the tasks I have before me. Try to put yourself in my shoes and treat me as you would like to be treated if the situations were reversed.

Will the Real Professional Please Stand?

It doesn't matter how many letters people can list after their name. I'm sure it's a consideration when it comes to the amount they're paid. I also have to commend people for all the time and effort they've put into attaining that degree. When it comes to the way I'm treated as a contributing member of a team to make decisions about my child's education and welfare, however, the letters don't mean diddly-squat.

I've found professional people who didn't have all the titles to go with their names who treated me in a very professional manner. The following list details how good professionals act.

- They don't make judgments about me based on what other people say.

- They come to meetings on time.

- They don't talk about other cases during their meeting with me.

- They don't reject my ideas.

- They don't assume my child can't learn.

- They recognize my child's strengths.

- When giving me bad news, they do it tactfully, with compassion, and privately (if possible).

- They don't have to take time to read through their files during the meeting to find out who the meeting is about.

- They don't assume that their way is the only way.

- They don't try to force issues.

- They will admit they're wrong or that they don't have the answer.

- They don't pretend to have experience or know how to deal with an issue if they don't.

- They are flexible.

- They don't try to rush through a meeting.

- They don't continually glance at their watch.

- They are honest with me.

- They are aware of my rights, and they let me know what they are.

- They don't try to impress me with their titles.

- They don't resent my input.

- They truly care about children.

All professionals ought to act in this manner, but it's one of those sad facts of life that they don't. One of the most professional people I know is Krystal's aide. I have no idea what amount of education she has, but she is respectful of Krystal and me. She's very conscientious and kind. I think genuine kindness should be displayed by all people who deal with the public.

Krystal's pediatrician is also a person who treats me with a great deal of respect. He always gives me credit for being able to care for her. He would let me choose whether to hospitalize her when it wasn't too serious. He follows up on all the questions I ask him, and he will admit to not having all the answers.

Both of these people act professionally. If either of them made a suggestion that I found questionable, I would have to question my reasons before rejecting it. I'd probably do what they suggested because I don't have all the answers either. They both have given me reason to trust them.

Look Through the Windows of My World

You can't walk a mile in my shoes, but you can take a short journey with me, and I can show you some scenes from my life. I don't ordinarily open up to strangers like this, but you're not really a stranger. You're the person responsible for my child's education. You may be a superintendent, a principal, a teacher, a guidance counselor, or a special education director. It doesn't matter. I'll probably be discussing things with you sometime during the course of my child's education. The object of this is not to make you feel sorry for me. Far from it. It's to try to help you understand me and my child. If you can understand something about the places I've been, you may be able to understand where I'm coming from today. So let's get started. You may learn something.

This first window shows you a death. It's not a typical death. We didn't get flowers or have calling hours. It was a very private affair and not too many people even realized it at the time. This was the death of a dream.

You see, I always thought I'd grow up, marry, and have a couple of normal children. When this death occurred, and it doesn't matter whether it happened when my child was first born or as he began to develop, it's still basically the same. My whole life changed. I hadn't planned to have a child who had to use a wheelchair or who would never be able to hear or see or pass a standard IQ test. I was forced to change my whole outlook on the future. It may have taken awhile to go through all the stages I had to go through to get to where I am today. There was grief. A lot of it. There was a lot of denial too. The doctors had to be wrong. Maybe the denial came before the grief.

I don't really remember. It doesn't make a whole lot of difference. I had to get through those two stages before I could accept what had happened and learn to accept my child and the limitations he would put on my dreams. I had to come up with a new dream.

This next window shows me after I've learned to accept my child for who he is. I've learned to take all the backward glances and tasteless remarks in stride. I've seen ignorance from people I thought were intelligent, and I've met some really wonderful people I never would have known had my child been normal. I've had to learn how to make people understand that my child is a child first, with a disability second.

I've seen miracles too. I've seen the first step the doctors said would never happen, and I've seen the light of recognition in my child's eyes when he finally grasped the meaning of something. I've seen sunsets you wouldn't believe once I had to really look at them and describe them to my blind child. What may seem ordinary has taken on a whole new significance for me.

I've learned a whole new language. It's called "medical-ese." Doctors tend to speak in words you don't hear every day. At first, I thought I'd never be able to keep all the terms and isms straight, but I conquered it and speak it fairly fluently now. I'm beginning to learn "teacher-ese" now. Teachers use a lot of abbreviations and numbers, but I know I can learn the language. Even though I've accepted my child, this next window will show you my fears for my child's future. I realize it's going to take a lot more effort if my child is to lead a fulfilling life. Learning may be difficult for him—and in some cases, impossible—but I've really been trying to make his life as normal as possible. I try to focus on the abilities he has, and I do my best to make him feel worthwhile.

I realize there are some things that my child can't yet do, and he may never be able to do some things. I tend to focus too much on what he can do and not what he can't do, but this helps me and my family. I sometimes seem to be taking three steps backward for every one forward. Maybe I do tend to attach more significance to his accomplishments than I should.

You may see only the bad things about my child. It may not seem fair to you if you have to spend more time with him or do things differently for one child when you have a classroom full of children who learn things in standard ways. My child may always be disrupting your class and may not seem to be learning much. I don't expect you to ignore other students for his sake, but I really don't want him shoved in a back classroom with all the other different kids either. He may have to spend some time in a smaller classroom with more individual attention. My goal is to make his life as normal as I possibly can, and being around regular kids helps. It will take some understanding on both our parts to work this out. Perhaps some of your brighter students could help my child in some areas. You'll be teaching them about responsibility, and they'll learn acceptance and values that you're not even responsible for teaching. They'll view children with disabilities as children first and disabled second. In many cases, they'll learn to accept my child before you will.

As a parent, I know I'm not perfect. I make mistakes every day. I realize teachers are only human. I also remember the time when some of my teachers were up there with God in my estimation. They had such an impact on my life. It was a shock to find out they led ordinary lives outside of the classroom. I've become more realistic as far as my opinions go. Your lives probably aren't as worry-free or stress-free as I used to think, and my child may only add to a day that's too full and too underpaid. If you at least make the effort to try to treat my child as a person, I know how he will view you. Sit next to God for a while.

My attitude may not be the best you've seen lately. I may already have had some run-ins with the system before I ever talk to you. I may come on too forcefully and seem too demanding. Maybe I've had to be to get services for my child. Maybe my sister-in-law has excluded my child and me from every family get-together she's had since I've had a disabled child. Maybe my husband isn't supportive. Or maybe the professionals I've dealt with before have done everything they could to help me. Maybe I'll assume that you will too, and I won't remember all the hard lessons I've learned along the way. Or I may remember each one too vividly. It may be a combination of all these feelings. Whatever the case, I am just a normal person who wants the best for my child, and I'm just trying to make up for the things I feel he justly deserves.

I probably already know that my son won't be the captain of the football team and my daughter won't be homecoming queen, but that doesn't mean that I don't have dreams for them. I've just substituted other dreams for those I've lost. We all harbor some pretty unrealistic expectations for our children, and I'm no different from any other parent.

If I seem to want too much from you, I don't mean to. I may have a lot on my mind, or I may not have really accepted the direction my life has taken. It sometimes takes years for a parent to get to that point of acceptance. Maybe my planned future keeps intruding. That's really not too hard to understand when you realize that I lived with that dream for most of my life, whereas I've lived with my reality for a lot shorter period. I may even be feeling cheated because my life seems so different from yours. There may be a lot of resentment in me, or I could just be tired of fighting the battle. Maybe I hated driving in that old car, but I decided when my child was born that I'd quit working and stay home with him. Home was where I felt I was needed most. You may have a better education than me, and you may feel more qualified to make decisions about how and what my child will learn. In most cases, you are the expert and I will (try to) bow to your judgment. But if you feel I'm realistic and I've accepted my child's limitations, there will be instances when I will know what will work best. In that case, I am the expert. I've had an education and had to learn things you should be thankful you've never had to learn.

If you take all the things you've seen through my windows into consideration, you may understand me and my child better. If we work together, maybe we can do what I pray for each night. That is to give my child as many opportunities as possible to lead a normal life in a world that doesn't always seem fair.

This open letter is not representative of all parents of children with disabilities, but I've tried to make it a fair sampling of the views I've heard expressed from other parents and from various articles I've read. I know I won't live to see utopia, and my children probably won't either, but the laws that are being passed today providing inclusion of children with disabilities into public schools will give educators the opportunity to make this a generation of better people. And that's one step closer!

I'd Rather Be Anywhere But Here

Stop and think for a moment about conversations you have had with parents. Do you ever feel that they're not the best meetings you have to attend? Do you ever feel that perhaps the parents are hostile or that they don't seem to want to be there? Do you take it personally? Or do you feel that it's just another meeting that will go nowhere? Do you ever feel uncomfortable around parents if they get emotional? Do you wish they would just stick to the business at hand and leave all that personal stuff out?

My experience as a parent and parent mentor has given me the opportunity to witness some professional reactions to parents. One of the most common statements I hear is that they don't care. The truth is we care too much. Another fact is that we'd rather be anywhere else when we have to have meetings with you. It's not because you're terrible people. You're just doing your job, and we really shouldn't hold that against you. But the fact remains that if our children had been born typical, we wouldn't even have to know you.

Many times, as I lay awake at night, I think how much easier it would be for me to get along without an arm or a leg than it is to have to deal with a child who receives special education services. I'd give up many, many things in my life if only my child would be okay. I'm sure other parents feel much the same way. We truly would cut off our own arms to make this problem go away, and in the long run, that would be much easier to adjust to.

I lost a lot of things when I entered the special education arena. I lost my dream for the all-American family. I also had to give up a whole bunch of time for myself because these kids don't just take up more of your time. They take up all of your time and influence it in ways you can't imagine. They change it on an ongoing basis. While you can get away from it all during summer vacation, it's only intensified for me.

So, in all honesty, I have to say that I wish I'd never met you. If I would have never had to have met you, it would mean that maybe my life would be a little more like I'd dreamed it would be. So it's not you I don't want to be around. It's what you stand for. The one thing I still have control over is how I act in public. There are two things that can make me react in ways I hate. One is the person who thinks my child belongs somewhere else and as if they chose to be different and don't deserve a typical childhood. These people start most meetings with a list of all the things my child can't do. Believe me, you're not telling me anything I don't already know. These people make me angry. They are being paid to facilitate my child's education. I get to do it for nothing and at a much higher emotional cost. When I get angry, I usually show the hostility I feel about the whole situation. When my emotions get tapped, it's hard to say how much of what I feel is directed at what you may have said specifically or at the whole situation in general. You may not even realize that you've made me angry, because single words or phrases may trigger reactions that I don't have a whole lot of control over. You have to remember that I already might have a history of "bad" encounters to draw from, especially if my child's disability has been apparent since birth.

The other reaction I hate is when I get all teary eyed when someone does or says something very nice. The sad fact is that society has an easier time ignoring our children's problems than they do dealing with them. When parents are faced with a truly compassionate person, it can sometimes be a so-good-it-makes-you-cry type of situation.

Right now, I imagine you're thinking, "Boy, we can't win with this person!" Not so. You can make me feel more comfortable at this meeting. I realize that you can't truly understand the challenges I face. I've read about breast cancer and AIDS and child abuse. I know all the right words, but I don't really understand the emotions people go through when they face these things. I can only imagine the heartbreak these people must feel. I do understand the heart-wrenching emotions I felt when I learned my daughter was blind. If you could have felt my pain for only a moment when that happened, you'd be amazed that I survived it and you'd treat me with a lot more respect.

I think it all boils down to that one word: respect. If you can respect my position and value me for being able to cope with an impossible, no-win situation, it would mean a lot. Don't criticize me for not doing as much as I should. I'm doing what I can, and the fact that I'm not locked up in a mental institution is evidence of that. Tell me what my child is doing well, and think of some ways that we can build on that to help in areas that he might not be doing so well in.

Respect my culture. Realize that geography, heredity, and economic situations might affect my life in ways I don't choose for them to. We were faced with a situation in the past where the only way at the time for us to be able to have health insurance coverage would be if I divorced my husband and went on welfare. Luckily, we were able to get coverage without taking these steps and it was an option we only had to consider, but we did seriously consider it. When you're raised to believe that if you try hard enough and you're willing to work that it will be okay, facing that situation was unbelievably hard. I'm not mad at you; sometimes, I'm just mad at the world.

When you hear all this talk about team players and collaboration, it's hard for parents and professionals alike. We each have our own experiences to draw on.

We're being asked to dance, but we're listening to different songs.

Chapter Ten

For Parents

The articles written in this chapter were written for various publications over a span of many years. Not all of them are specifically about my children. Some of them may reference "he" rather than "she" to appeal to a wider audience.

Bad Days

Who said life had to be fair? I realize my life did not come with a guarantee of happiness and success.

But even knowing this, I still have days when I resent other people's normal lives. I rant and rave about the injustice of having two atypical kids and the way my life has turned out.

I long for that normal life, and I wish my biggest problem of the day were which dance studio to choose for the girls' dancing lessons or what dress to wear to the church social. On these days, I wish my kids belonged to anyone but me. I did nothing to deserve this!

After I've ranted and raved it all out of my system, though, I stop and think back to when my life was normal. I still had bad days, but the things I worried about were whether my car was clean and if all the weeds were pulled out of the cracks in the sidewalk, and why so-and-so hadn't returned my call?

In retrospect, these worries were all so trivial. At least now I have legitimate reasons to be upset. We're talking about social injustice, poor professional attitudes, and no health insurance. These are issues that mean something, and the decisions I make will have some pretty far-reaching effects for my children.

My good friend Jennifer is so upset because her hair stylist cut her hair too short, and it doesn't flatter her. She's sure people will be staring at her for weeks. I could shave my head, and people would still notice my kids first. I might be a tiny bit upset over a bad haircut, but I wouldn't have the time to agonize over it like she is doing. There really are more important things to consider in my life.

I suppose I should be thankful that there is more depth to my life now, and some days, I am very aware of how the abnormal has changed my perspective and priorities for the better. I don't have time anymore to make life miserable for my husband, and I'm too busy to worry about the social structure in my community. I don't even have time to keep up with *Days of Our Lives* anymore.

Some days, I am very aware of my change in attitude about some of the more important things in life, and I thank God that I've come to be like this. But the biggest fact I realize about all this is that I am *not* a super mom. I can only do so much, and the days when I do rant and rave are normal. I am allowed to feel this way, and I'm not a bad mother because of it. It's a normal reaction to the stresses that a developmentally or physically handicapped child places upon a person. I'm not a bad person because I feel this way sometimes. I'm only human, and I really think I am the best mother my kids could have.

The Silent, Constant Scream

Parents who have kids with disabilities usually seem to be fairly normal people. People who don't have children with disabilities sometimes tell us what saints we must be to do all the things we do. Those of us who have been at this for several years know we're not saints. We know how long it took us to get to this place—a place where we appear to be capable and normal.

Each of us deals with the disability issue in different ways. Some accept it as God's way. Others accept it as a challenge to grow. Some are angry. Some are sad. Most of us bounce back and forth between all these feelings.

We each cope in different ways. Some advocate. Some scream. Some hide behind humor. Some silently accept. Some use their spouses (or some other close person) as whipping boys. It's a mixed up, jumbled up mess whenever you try to figure out what or how you are handling this.

Most of us never actually figure it out. We just continue to plod along, overcoming each new obstacle as it arises. We never fully understand exactly what it is that drives us. Perhaps it's better that we don't know. Sometimes I have moments of startling clarity. The other night, while talking to a bunch of friends, someone said that it was okay to scream. Most did their best jungle scream, but I couldn't. The conversation had been about kids and Christmas. I shared with this group that Christmas was the worst for me because my younger daughter couldn't see all the lights. Her blindness always seems worst during this season. The full impact of blindness and all it entails really tears at my heart.

Suddenly, I knew that there is a silent, constant scream within me. I do my best to muffle its vibrations. I keep busy. I do what has to be done. I advocate. I write. I try to keep the scream buried. I fear that if I do scream, I will never be able to stop.

Some people may say that I still haven't totally accepted my child's disability. Maybe I haven't. Maybe I never will. Maybe the scream is my way of not accepting. Who knows?

Many of you will understand what I am trying to convey. I'm sure many adults with disabilities also have the silent scream within. It's caused by all the unfairness and frustration that tags along with disabilities. It's the force, the adrenaline, the vibration that keeps us moving, whether it be of mind or body. It can be channeled into constructive areas, or it can lead straight to destruction. The person who feels it must make a choice to scream aloud or silently.

The Answer

I'm always looking for the answer. If I could only have someone give it to me, I'm sure life would be simpler. But as I sit here typing away, trying to figure this out, I realize that the answer will always elude me. Am I saying that there is no answer? No, it's not that at all.

The problem lies in the question. And the question keeps changing.

Take the question that all parents who have children with problems ask: "Why me?" I asked that question a lot. I asked it until I was hoarse. I dreamt about it. I had nightmares about that question. I begged to understand the reasoning behind the decision to give these children to me. Then, one day in the grocery store as people tried to unobtrusively (but unsuccessfully) get a really good look at my younger daughter to see if she really were blind, another question replaced the original: "Why not me?"

As I wheeled my way down the aisle, glancing at products on the shelves and singing nonsense words to my daughter, I knew that there was no one else in the world who could love this little baby as much as I did. There was no one else who would feel so defensive and protective. If she had to be shielded from these rude people, I would do it, and I would do it better than anyone else.

Then there was the day not too long ago when she got those little hands on my face, held it still, zoomed in until we were nose to nose, and asked, "Why do you leave us at a babysitter's and teach STEP (Systematic Training for Effective Parenting) classes?"

"Well," I replied, "I go to try to teach other mommies how to be better mommies and to remind myself to be a better mommy."

"But you're already a better mommy," she responded.

What could I do? A silent tear of gratitude trickled down my cheek. I hugged her tightly. I knew this moment would be filed along with all those other memorable ones I keep in my heart.

This seems like a fitting epitaph for a life: "She was a better Mommy." Me, the person whose goal it is to have an impressive obituary, would be content with this on my headstone. But why not do more? Why not add to it?

I know I keep harping on how our children can make us better people. I know it can be hard for new parents to realize the blessing they've received when they learn their child may have a disability. Maybe it's a mixed blessing, because they also screw our lives up pretty badly.

They make it harder to go to the grocery store. They make it harder to cope. They make us rethink our entire value system. They make us cry. They make us grow. They keep us on the edge of fatigue. They make us learn to love better.

So, for my children and for myself, I will keep trying to be a better mommy. I will also try to be a better person. I will continue to write in the hope that I can help other parents realize that they are not alone with their fears and questions. As I exorcise my demons, I hope to bring to light the full spectrum of emotions we face. Thank you all for reading what I write. Thanks to my kids for raising the question in the first place. I will keep asking it in many different ways and probably for the rest of my life. The day I quit asking will be the day they start writing my obituary.

Take My Hand

"But if you'll take my hand, my son, my son, all will be well when the day is done." It was easy for Peter, Paul, and Mary to say that. None of them had kids with disabilities. But they also said "you will inherit what mankind has done," which is all too true when it comes to having kids with disabilities.

Television portrays only beautiful people, and it has only been recently that you see kids who are different in commercials and on *Sesame Street* and *Barney*. It's about time someone noticed that people with disabilities are people too!

I'm a person who lives with my kids 365 days a year. I'm the one who tries to believe that all professionals are noble and dedicated. I'm also the one who has learned to appreciate the small successes and to celebrate them. I'm the eternal dreamer, and I want to believe that when I'm gone, the world will be a better place for my kids to live in.

On the whole, my kids don't have it too bad. I've been the general of this battle for quite a while now, and I have learned a few techniques that have helped.

Plus, many of the people I work with share their strategies, so it's not as though I'm completely alone or the only parent in the world who is faced with these problems. There are a multitude of parents out there who are fighting the same battles, along with people in high places who make the policies that protect our kids.

I'm concerned about all the other parents who are going through the same thing. It's not easy to be the minority in 99 percent of the dealings you have. Having a child with a disability is a big enough problem in itself. And when you have to not only deal with the disability on a personal level, but also on a larger level that involves communities, schools, and systems, it can become overwhelming.

There are days when I'd just like to lie down and die and pass the battle banner to someone who's not so weary of fighting. I suppose I could just sit back and let the system do what it would, but I know I couldn't live with myself if I did. I'd feel I was doing nothing to make my children's lives better, and being apathetic isn't my style anyway. So I do what any normal parent would do. I try to make the world a better place for my kids. I try to get rid of all the injustice and prejudice that is there waiting to attack them.

I know I can take it better than they can, especially at this stage in their lives. So I continue to fight. When an IEP meeting gets personal and I look like as good a target as anyone to attack, it does hurt, and I often cry, but I have to stick to my dreams. I have to remain committed to my cause, and I can't let them make me feel guilty because little Johnny's parents have complained about my child being included in the regular classroom.

There will always be people who are ready to blame me and my children for any inconvenience that arises. I can hope to change a portion of the minds out there, but I know there are some people who will always discriminate against my kids and whose minds I will never be able to change. I have to accept the fact that this world we live in is less than perfect and do what I can to make it better. For my own sake, I have to remember that all my victories don't have to be big ones. The little ones add up, so if I change one person's attitude, that makes this world one person better, and that's one more person on my side than I had yesterday.

Maybe it won't "all be well" when this day is done, but it will be a bit better. Being responsible for making some people question their prejudices, if only for a moment, is a change that needs to be made. It's about making friends for our kids and ourselves, but it's also about finding out who the worthwhile people really are.

So take my hand, my son, and let's try to change your inheritance.

Three Wishes

If I could have three wishes, the first one that comes to mind would be to make my kids typical—no disabilities, no problems. But that wish falls into the same category as being sixteen again and knowing as much as I do now. With the granting of the wish comes the loss of all you've learned.

I have met so many wonderful people over the years, and my whole view of life has changed. I'm not the same person. I'm a little wiser, more informed, and a lot fatter. (Two out of three isn't bad.) I feel more justified in taking up space on this planet. I've learned about real issues, and I've made changes that have affected others in positive ways.

I've gotten the chance to write, and it's meaningful writing. People are learning from my experiences, and my kids are doing okay. I don't yell at my husband as much because I have other causes to occupy me. I'm making a difference!

I wouldn't know Sonja (the early intervention specialist), Molly (the preschool teacher), Joan (the principal at the Developmental Disabilities Center), or Dotty (my kids' current teacher). It's also true that I wouldn't know the 4-H leader who said, "You'll have to become an advisor if you want your kids to be in this club." But then I also wouldn't have realized what a difference there was in her and the people at Brownies who just accepted them with no qualms.

I wouldn't know what a difference there can be in people. I'd think they were all the same, and I would have missed knowing how special some of them really are. I'd truly be less of a person today if I hadn't met these people. I'd probably be someone the me of today wouldn't want to know.

Maybe if I just wish for it to be all right to be different, it would be a better wish.

If My Kid Were Typical

Sometimes, as parents of children who are different, we often feel as if life has dealt us an unfair blow. We've had to rearrange our lives and dreams to accommodate the unique needs of these little people.

It's rarely convenient or easy, and it's very common to focus on the negative. Speaking for myself, I've gained quite a few things from my children though. First of all, I've met some truly remarkable people. I've made some friends I wouldn't trade for the world. (And compared to some of the ones I had before, they're really an improvement!)

I've learned to value individuals for their strengths, and I've learned a whole lot about human nature. I know what compassion really means. I've seen miracles, and I don't waste my time worrying about trivial things. I've learned the language of education and medicine and have even been mistaken for a medical professional by another medical professional.

I've been in the position to help others in a truly significant way, and my values are definitely higher than they previously were. I have solid dreams, and I'm not so easily swayed by trends. I feel as if I'm making a difference in many, many lives. And I've learned how beautiful the world is, as I've explained sunsets to my blind daughter. I've learned to see things differently as I've painstakingly figured out why my autistic daughter reasons the way she does.

I've been through some scary times too, but they've only taught me that I can do things I never thought possible.

Chapter Eleven

What Is Important

When my children were very young, I attended a parenting class. It literally saved my sanity and changed the way I felt about and reacted to other things going on in my life. I eventually even became a trainer for the program and taught several parenting classes myself.

It's been many years since then, and the three main things I learned from it were to choose your battles, speak softly, and break down what you expect into easy-to-understand steps.

Prior to attending the parenting class, I was forever yelling and screaming at Kimberly for everything from unrolling the toilet paper to scattering her toys all over the house. I don't think she heard a word I was yelling at her. I would catch myself thinking, "Who are you?" I wasn't a screamer, nor was anyone in my family.

The parenting class taught me to choose what was most important to correct about her behavior. I had to choose two or three behaviors and correct her only about those things. Forget all the rest. I chose to focus on removing the safety plugs from the outlets and running away. Pretty soon, Kimberly began to pay more attention to me when

I did get upset with her because that tone of voice was different from my normal one. She actually listened!

I also found that a lower tone of voice—you know, a deep, serious type—would get more of a response than yelling would. I'm not saying that I quit yelling completely. When she got too far away, I had to just yell so she could hear me. At any rate, those strategies worked. I also praised her for good behavior. It's always stymied me that children misbehave to seek attention. Well, they get our attention, but in a way that doesn't make much sense to me, but who's to say? It's way more difficult to remember to praise them than you might think. We expect them to know that what they are doing is right. Get into the habit of praising your kids for good behavior. It doesn't cost a thing.

I found that the very same strategies worked with all sorts of situations. It proved especially helpful at IEP meetings. I would choose the top three services I wanted on the plan and work to get them implemented. Many times, a personal educational aide is what a parent wants for their child. By far, it is the last thing the school wants to provide. It's one of the most costly things you can ask for. So if getting an aide for your child is what you really want, you might need to work up to that gradually. Ask for a smaller class size, which has an aide who works with all the children. Ask for tutoring. Ask for reduced assignments. There are any number of things you can ask for that can help your child. Document all of this. If it works, that's great. If it doesn't, then you can show proof that the modifications and accommodations haven't helped.

If the school sees that you can be reasonable, it is more likely to give you what you want. If administrators buy into the plan, that's even better. The ideal situation is for parents and teachers to work together. I have actually had it happen on many occasions. When the system works, it benefits everyone.

We all have the ideal plan in our minds of what we see as the ideal future for our kids. When my kids were younger, the educators would always ask at IEP meetings what my vision for my kids was. I would sometimes look at them like they were from some strange planet. How was I supposed to have a vision when getting through a week of tantrums and doctor appointments was all I could deal with? At times, my mind couldn't even begin to comprehend a future for them. But the beauty of visions is that they can change and grow with us. Once you learn how to envision a week, then you can go on to a month and then a year. Pretty soon, the future will peek at you.

The future you see may not be something you're willing to share with professionals. Maybe you think they will just laugh at you. Then again, maybe your vision comes with too much baggage to share with others. You may think, "I want them to be liked, and I want my sister-in-law to treat them better, and I wish they could have a pony, and I wish they would act better in public and I wish ..." The list goes on and on and on. It may be hard to pick just one thing. That's when you go back to the important things or those things that will help them achieve some of those wishes on your list. Maybe you just want Johnny to be able to play with his peers. Focus on that. Maybe through those skills, he will learn to act better in public and maybe (just maybe) your sister-in-law will treat him a little better. Okay, so the sister-in-law thing is a long shot, but you see what I mean?

Learn to think outside the box.

An example is about a young boy who had Asperger syndrome. He absolutely loved to talk about all the movies he watched. Socially, he was having a difficult time with other kids. They really didn't want to hear about those movies all the time. I suggested that he be given an assignment to report on one movie a week. He would have to research it (figure out the beginning, middle, and end), write about it (spelling, sentence structure, and punctuation), and give a report to the class about that movie. That would be his time to shine when everyone would be listening to him. Plus, he would also be learning necessary skills and be graded on them.

Chapter Twelve

Telling Your Story

You may think telling your story would be easy. You have so many great things you can tell people about your kids. We all like to talk about the cute things our kids do. You may even have some not so great things to say about how other people or family members are dealing with your child's disability. Unless you're the paid speaker at a conference, you need to condense your story.

I know people who can start a sentence, and five minutes later, they're still talking, and you've forgotten what the point of the story was. When you're in meetings with professionals, you have limited time to get your point across. Avoid he-said-she-said types of stories that just add unnecessary words to the point you're trying to make.

Sometimes the facts are enough. Professionals speak in levels and statistics, and they understand them. There are times when a short story can help you elaborate on some aspect of your child's disability. Let me share with you two stories I have about my oldest daughter Kim.

Kim tends to take the things you say very literally. And I mean *very* literally!

One day she was standing next to our back door. Her dad said, "Let the dog out. He wants to go outside."

Kim just stood there. Her dad repeated the request. Again, Kim just stood there. The dog was prancing around, and her dad was beginning to get upset. In a much louder voice, he said, "What's the problem? Why won't you let the dog out? He wants to go outside."

Kim very calmly looked at him and said, "We don't have a boy dog."

She was right. Our dog was a female.

Another time, when I had an evening class I had to attend and my husband was out of town, I asked a neighbor if Kim could come over to her house when it got dark. By that time, Kim was old enough and capable enough to be on her own for a few hours. I left home and told Kim that she could stay home until it started to get dark and then she could go over to Vivien's. Kim said she would.

When I got home several hours later, it was completely dark.

I pulled into Vivien's drive and went to the house to get Kim. When Vivien answered the door, she said Kim wasn't there. My house was completely dark, but I drove over just to check. No Kim. Where was she? I was beginning to panic. I drove back to the neighbor's to ask if she'd noticed any suspicious activity around our house.

We were standing just outside her door, and lo and behold, here comes Kim strolling out of the dark of the woods behind Vivien's house.

"Where have you been?" I shouted. "I thought I told you to come over here when it got dark!"

"I did," said Kim. "I was out in Vivien's woods watching for deer."

Duh! I didn't say, "Go over to Vivien's house. Knock on the door and go *inside*." In her mind, Kim had done exactly what I told her to do. My point about Kim being very literal has been made.

Krystal's visual impairment pretty much speaks for itself, but I do have one story about her that helps remind people to explain to her about the things around her that she can't see. People tend to think that if they tell her there's a tree on the road that she will understand that the tree probably fell there and that trees aren't supposed to be on roads.

Krystal and her dad watch television together. He watches a lot of vehicle-related shows such as drag racing, farm shows, tractor pulls, and all sorts of stuff like that.

She's been watching those types of shows with him for years. He tells her what's going on, and we think we're the master parents of descriptive communication.

One day, while watching tractor pulls on RFD, a television channel devoted to rural issues, concerns, and interests, Krystal asks, "Dad, why do people want to pull tractors anyway? Aren't you supposed to drive them?"

Get it? Tractor pulls. Not people driving tractors trying to pull heavy loads. We need to work more on our descriptive communication skills.

Think about something that has happened that highlights or presents a true picture of your child. Make it short enough so people will listen without wondering if the story would ever end. Leave out the family dynamics. No one cares what your mother-in-law said or that your child acts just like his Uncle Jim.

Back-to-School (with Instructions): A Student Portfolio

When Kim entered high school, it meant going to a new building with all new teachers. It was a huge change for her. The school presented us with a one-page IEP. It was as if they planned to wait and see what would happen and then deal with it. It didn't seem like much of a plan to me, so I created a PowerPoint presentation on how to make a student portfolio that people could share with new staff.

It's that time of year again. The kids will soon be back in the classroom. If your child is in the process of moving to a new building and you're facing the prospect of new teachers who don't know your child, a new building administration with an unknown personality, and possibly the addition of new children from other schools, it can be a terrifying venture for the kids and parents.

My older daughter, Kim, will be entering high school at the end of August. We ended last year without signing the IEP. They proposed a one-page, very vague IEP and said she would take the regular proficiency test. Very politely I said she wouldn't be capable of that since she doesn't read and hasn't been exposed to most of that material. Plus, the stress for her would be overwhelming. I offered to work with her teacher and come up with some reasonable goals and objectives, which I did. I checked with the special education director, who said the goals seemed reasonable, and sent them back to the school. The school sent back my goals and objectives with a cover sheet for me to sign. The only problem was that they'd failed to fill out who, where, how often, etc. I didn't sign it. It was decided that we would meet with all the teachers a week or so before school started to fill in the missing pieces and get the IEP signed.

That works for me. Teachers will know what they are teaching, where they are teaching it, and the schedule will be in place. If there have been any staff changes, it will be helpful for those new teachers to be part of this process.

However, I am still concerned about how they will react to her. Her IEP goals and objectives are quite detailed, but I'm not sure that the IEP alone will give them an accurate picture of Kim. They won't know about the amazing progress she has made over the years or that this kid with an IQ in the forties can appropriately and consistently use "dollar" words, or words you would not expect a person with an IQ of 40 to use, in her conversations. A few examples: I fell off a step ladder the other day. She asked if I was injured. She will say, "This is the pig's snout," or "I know my attitude wasn't appropriate."

I decided to present them with a more detailed account of Kim. It will be her portfolio and will highlight her accomplishments and her shortcomings in a way the IEP and testing reports cannot. I thought a long time about the format I wanted to use. I finally decided to use a notebook, with dividers that would be quick and easy to reference.

I also wanted it to be something that Kim could understand and explain about herself so I've added a few pictures that will cue her to what it's about. The actual portfolio will probably have more pictures with captions. You can add medical information if it's appropriate and some information on your child's specific disability. Samples of homework are also a good idea.

You will need to decide exactly what and how you want to present your own child's information.

The first page is titled "Meet Kim," and it has two pictures of her. The next page is titled "Kim's Intro."

Kim's Intro Page

Kim is a unique child. She has many skills that may not be apparent when you first meet her. Kimberly, now a teenager, was diagnosed with autism at age six. She has pretty fragmented skills. She can learn to do things if she wants to, but more importantly, she needs to have all the pieces of information to make it meaningful for her. If it doesn't interest her, though, and doesn't connect with some information she already has, you might as well forget it.

I've seen her read phrases, but she's unable to repeat them. The concept of tomorrow is getting easier for her, but the concept of next week is still hard for her.

She's come a long, long way from the little girl who literally climbed up your leg at the sound of a mixer, vacuum, fire alarm, or siren, and she no longer hides under the table when things get hectic. She interacts with other kids and goes to all her classes by herself. Kim loves animals. She has a cockatiel, a German shepherd, three llamas she shows, and some cats.

She used to love to play with hand puppets, and you would find yourself having a conversation with her puppet, rather than Kim, if you weren't careful. We've tried very hard to do away with the puppets and replace them with more appropriate communication, but it used to be the only way you could communicate with her. She will still revert to it if she is under a lot of stress. Kim has a younger sister, Krystal, who is blind. It makes it a bit difficult as far as appropriate peer interaction goes since there are some things Krystal cannot do with Kim. Right now, Kim's biggest problem is being a teenager and the attitude that seems to go along with it.

Mom and Dad can deal with the autism, but this teenage thing can be a bit difficult. Her mental ability may be lower than her chronological age, but her attitude is pure fifteen year old.

Author's note: Kim is twenty-eight now. She graduated with her class in 2004, but did not leave the school system until 2007.

Least Restrictive Environment

Kim began attending school in this district when she was in kindergarten. She attended preschool at Golden Rule, which was our county's school that served children with disabilities. Since Kim is not always able to distinguish appropriate behavior, we decided long ago to have her attend a typical school where she would be exposed to more normal behavior.

Over the years, Kim has been included in regular classes with some time in the resource room. There have been times when the inclusion has been beneficial and times when she has just been there. While we understand that Kim needs a more functional curriculum, we also feel that inclusion, whenever possible, is the best choice for her. She picks up information you may not initially think she has the ability to understand. The benefit to her far outweighs the inappropriate behavior she picks up when exposed to other children with special needs, especially those with behavior problems. If she spends the majority of her school day with students who may have inappropriate behavior, she will have more behavior problems.

Kim has the capability to live and work in the regular world, so we feel she needs to be educated in it whenever possible with the proper supports and services necessary to make it a positive learning experience for her.

Transition Skills

Kim needs to learn skills that will benefit her as she moves into adulthood. She already has many social skills. She can go into a restaurant and order a meal with no problem. She knows to tip the waitress, but if she had a twenty and a five, she might leave the twenty as a tip and try to pay with the five.

Kim had an office job at the middle school. She put labels on newsletters for the secretary, had an ID, and received actual money for her work. She received a "paycheck" and cashed it at the office. We provided the money for her pay, and we will continue to do that if she is able to have a job this year.

Kim works well with animals and small children. She follows directions if there aren't too many steps involved. Once she learns a task, she can be counted on to perform it correctly.

She has fair social skills but may be overly affectionate to people, especially teachers she likes. She knows it isn't appropriate to hug people in school, but she may need to be reminded of that.

Academics

Kim is a nonreader. She has good computer skills and can find the games hidden in the software.

Over the years, various reading programs have been used to teach Kim to read. She basically memorizes the programs and often appears to be able to read, but she cannot transfer those skills beyond the program.

She knows what billboards stand for, even if she can't read the words. She can properly identify products in the grocery store and tell you what traffic signs mean. Kim loves books. She has several she takes with her when we go places. One is a bird book with pictures and descriptions of many different birds. She can identify the majority of the birds in it. Some of them are books that have more words than pictures. She seems to want so much to read, and I believe she has some reading skills, but just not all the pieces.

Kim has a phenomenal memory. She can tell you about events that happened years ago, but may say they happened just the other day. She can recite whole movies verbatim. She is the finder of lost things at our house.

Social

Kim is involved in many different activities. She takes gymnastics lessons. She is in 4-H, where she has cats, birds, dogs, llamas, and photography as projects. She was in track last year. She enjoys being outside and collecting feathers, rocks, sticks, and bugs.

She has a few friends, but has a difficult time relating in a group. When kids make a conscious effort to include her, she does participate, but usually does not interact well in groups. If she has friends over who stay overnight, there will be a point where Kim will go outside or down to the basement to be alone for a while.

She attends many llama shows during the spring and summer. She has made a great deal of progress showing her llamas over the past three years, but still has a difficult time concentrating on the llama and the judge at the same time. She gets confused on the obstacle course, but has placed over typical kids a few times.

Future Plans

We picture a future for Kim where she will be a contributing member of society. We hope that she will have her own home and possibly a family. Financially, a home will be possible. A job will be necessary for the structure it will provide. Will it happen? I think it is possible with some help. It won't be a typical life. There will need to be some support, but we have seen tremendous growth with Kim. As she matures, we hope some more of the pieces of information she needs will fall into place.

We can expose her to as many situations as possible and hope for the best, prepare for the worst, and teach her as many skills as we can. If we focus on her strengths and develop them, we believe she will have a promising future. Kim has potential if we can only find a way to maximize it. As parents, we want the best for her and realize that our vision for her future will evolve and change over the next few years. We will do what we must to ensure that she is safe and happy.

In the meantime, let me share a story with you.

There was a young lady with mental and emotional problems far too numerous to mention. One of the main problems she had was that she was obsessed with smelling people's feet.

The team that was involved with her supported living had just about given up on finding a job for her. They'd discussed a job in a shoe store but felt it would place the temptation to smell feet much too close for comfort.

After a brainstorming session, they finally came up with a job that would suit this young woman perfectly. Can you guess what it was?

She could work in a shoe repair shop. She had the ability to be able to tag a pair of shoes and give the person a claim tag. The people could write their instructions on the tag that went on the shoes. When the shop wasn't busy, she could go in the back room and smell shoes to her heart's content. She just had to be taught that there are appropriate times and places for different behaviors, and her team felt it was a skill she could learn.

An excellent, creative team was able to work with this young woman and give her a future by working with her strengths and allowing her to be able to indulge in her inappropriate compulsion. That story gives me hope. We have far more to work with for Kim. In the meantime, I leave you with two quotes that give me hope.

> A glimpse is not a vision. But to a man on a mountain road
> at night, a glimpse of the next three feet of road may matter
> more than a vision of the horizon.
>> —C.S. Lewis

> We must accept finite disappointment, but we must never
> lose infinite hope.
>> —Unknown

Chapter Thirteen

People Will Be People

We've talked about laws and agencies. Now it's time to talk about the people we deal with. You will probably encounter many, if not all, of the types I will describe.

If you're lucky, you will encounter the compassionate doctor. This person will be honest with you and let you know about all the risks and benefits involved in anything you decide to do. They will give you the respect you deserve as a parent. They will understand your concerns. I was fortunate enough to have just such a doctor for Krystal and an equally supportive one for Kimberly.

Krystal's doctor was Dr. Schowinsky, and he involved me in all the decisions he made and was honest with me. Some of the specialists we visited over the years—and there were many of them—weren't always so wonderful. Maybe their bedside manner wasn't so hot, even if they were brilliant in their field, and maybe they tended to talk over my head. I always conducted research before our visits and hopefully asked semi-intelligent questions.

On the whole, most of our physician appointments were good. I truly respect those who actually listened to what I had to say. Doctors are probably the one population who have been the most professional in their dealings with me.

I haven't always been as happy with psychologists and psychiatrists. One we visited tested Kimberly while they were doing construction in an adjoining room, and he stopped the test after she missed being able to identify a park bench. We live in the country, and we'd never been to a city park. Now I realize that his stopping wasn't based on just that one answer, but the park bench question wasn't really fair. There is some basis, in my mind, that IQ tests aren't as accurate as they could be if you consider the many different cultures and lifestyles of people.

The principal at the school for the blind was a good enough guy. We got along pretty well with him, but at IEP time for the first few years, the question always came up as to what we did for our social time. Well, we live in the boonies. The closest major city is seventy-five miles from us. There are smaller towns, but nothing that compares to a large city. No bus you can hop on to go to town to see a movie. No subways. Our cultural opportunities are lacking to say the least! So we did 4-H. Lots of 4-H. And we did go to lots of llama shows. After the first year or two, he'd just say, "Oh, you do that 4-H thing."

The point of all that is that people do different things according to how they were raised, where they live, what they like, and what is available.

Over the years, I've been fortunate enough to have worked in the system, so I probably know more about how things work than the average parent. Let me explain that a bit so you'll understand.

My first job was with the Family Information Network, a state agency that provided support to families who had children from birth to three years of age with disabilities. I worked in several counties providing support to families and did presentations for them. The great part about that was that we had semimonthly meetings with all the other parents in the state who worked in that position, plus we received training on the laws and systems.

I then went to work with a statewide group that provided information and support to parents who had children in special education. That group was funded by a grant. I was an employee of the Educational Service Center (ESC), and I had a primary boss, but the special education directors and principals were also bosses of a sort.

My final job was with a statewide Parent Training Center, which was outside of the school district, but basically provided the same services as the previous jobs.

So over the years, I've had lots and lots of bosses. Some have been great. Others should never be allowed to be in charge of anything. You also have to realize that anyone you work with or have to interact with also has a life of their own, which may not always be so great. Maybe they have an alcoholic husband, their own kids are causing them problems, or they're dealing with financial issues. Maybe they're just having a bad day.

I've also seen some really great teachers who, when they became administrators, turned into tyrants. Holding any kind of power over people seemed to change their entire personalities.

The Peter Principle is a belief that, in an organization where promotion is based on achievement, success, and merit, that organization's members will eventually be promoted beyond their level of ability. Basically, employees tend to rise to their level of incompetence. People tend to have natural skills that work in one setting but not in others. This occurs in nearly all settings, so the people who are in charge may not be the best people for those jobs. It happens in every organization, and you can't blame the people because promotions usually come with raises. Who doesn't want to advance to higher pay?

Early in my career working with parents and professionals, I created a test for professionals. I had been a hair stylist, my husband did some drag racing, and we had horses at the time. It was just a simple match the term-and-definition test, but the theory behind it was to prove to professionals that parents are knowledgeable about many things that a professional may not know anything about. We can all bring skills to the table that come from our own experiences. When it comes to thinking outside of the box, a parent can be just as effective in coming up with ideas as a professional. The letters after a person's name don't guarantee that they know everything. Parents need to know that they can be productive and equal members of the team.

One of my favorite people was a dream to work for, but I've also seen her get overly defensive when parents were too demanding. When it becomes an issue of personalities rather than the real issues at hand, it can be nearly impossible to make any progress. We all have more than one side to us, and certain people seem to bring out the worst in us.

Maybe you're having a bad day, and the way you approached them caused their hackles to rise. Earlier, I talked about the llama judge who gave Krystal a special ribbon. Looking back, I'm sure that my reaction to the whole thing only made things worse. We were both right (at least in our own minds), and neither of us was going to concede anything. The whole issue was clouded with emotion rather than good sense.

My advice is to make a suggestion, hope they think about it for a bit, and then decide it was their idea to begin with. It may be the long way to solving a problem, but in the end, it's the best way. Rome wasn't built in a day, and neither are good relationships. It can take time, but if you try to find one thing you admire about a person, and if you can compliment them on it, it can change the whole course of your relationship.

You really need to read "Dealing with People You Can't Stand," the book I referenced earlier, to survive in this world if you're ever going to be able to get along. It helps you understand that the nature of the person, not you, can be a big part of how any interaction between you plays out.

Personally, I'm convinced that the whole world has autism and/or Asperger syndrome. Everyone has their own view of the world and how it should work. Much of the time, their principles and boundaries won't allow them to accept anything any different. You do things their way or it's the highway. This pretty much means you're screwed if you plan to disagree with them. Try to work around those people if you can. Approach your problem from a different angle. If that doesn't work, it may just be something you need to let go of and move on.

One of Krystal's teachers called me one time to say she felt Krystal was confused the year she attended two different schools during the week. One was a visually impaired unit in another district that she attended for three days of the week and the other was her home school district where she spent the other two days. She didn't feel Krystal belonged in her home school. It wasn't a pretty situation. However, a few years later, the same teacher told me that the way she taught when Krystal was in her class had helped the other children learn their ABCs easier, and more of the students became proficient in them sooner.

This applies to parents and professionals. If there's one thing I've learned through all of this, it's that you have to be flexible. Never say you would never do anything because, sure as the sun rises, you'll find yourself doing it.

Let's talk a bit about support. The support of your family is sometimes all you need. Then there are times when family support can be a real hindrance. If your family's culture—and I'm not talking about ethnicity here, just about the way they do certain things—are different from yours, you can have a big problem.

Some families disagree about things, get mad and fight, get over it and go on. Other families never acknowledge the elephant in the room and hope it will go away.

My mother, God rest her soul, was a great help to me. She bonded with Krystal and was always Krystal's favorite relative. She'd take Krystal on the weekends, and they always had a grand time. She was accepting of all Krystal's differences.

When it came to Kim, it was a different story. I don't think my mother ever truly bought into the fact that Kim couldn't always control her behavior. It was stressful to have to spend too much time around her with both girls. I always felt she thought I wasn't strict enough with Kim.

We did have one big blowup over the whole issue. When my sister got married, Kim took a huge hunk out of the wedding cake before it was time. I yelled. She yelled. I told her she would never see either of the girls again and left. The silence went on for a few weeks. I don't remember who called first, but we kissed and made up. But Kim became the elephant in the room that we never spoke about again.

So nothing is ever completely one way all the time. Being flexible and making the best of some situations is about all you can do sometimes.

My support came from friends and a few superhero professionals and colleagues. I could write another book about the professionals who helped us. Some of them were in our lives for only short periods of time, but they left lasting impressions. Much of the time, we lost contact with them because we moved on to different services and agencies as the girls got older. Some of them became and remain good friends.

Let me tell you about Albert. He was Krystal's Bureau of Services for the Visually Impaired counselor from the time she was small until she got out of school. He went to IEP meetings with me, helped us get special equipment for Krystal, and offered his advice whenever I asked. (And sometimes even when I didn't ask!)

I think he always appreciated the fact that we always put as much into any endeavor as we could. We'd purchase things on our own when we could and didn't keep calling to say Krystal needed this or that. Once she got out of school, Albert had either been promoted to another position or the agency went through a restructuring (which agencies seem to do a lot). Anyway, he was no longer able to work with Krystal. He arranged some training through his agency, and Krystal spent about a month at its training center.

Krystal didn't fare too well through that process. The agency said she wasn't mature enough for competitive employment. One job coach evaluator said she fondled her breasts and wouldn't obey rules. It was a terrible meeting with an agency that had always been awesome to work with. It was suggested that we have her spend some time at a workshop for people with disabilities to learn work skills until she was more mature.

We got her into a workshop, although it was difficult because she barely qualified because her functioning level was almost too high for that environment. However, the people worked with us and she got in.

We got involved with the Bureau of Services for the Visually Impaired again a few years later through a request from the workshop where she is now employed. That agency had a new program where her supports, strengths, and likes would be evaluated. The first evaluator pretty much fizzled out. I think there were some other things going on. We won't go into exactly what happened because I'm not entirely sure myself. I just had a gut feeling that things weren't going the way they should based on the explanation of how the program should work.

So I called Albert. He told me who does what and who I should call. I made the call, we got new people to evaluate her, and we're now close to ending that process.

I believe Krystal will get some financial help, and she'll be able to start her own business.

In a previous chapter, I said that agencies are imperfect. Much of how an agency works for you depends on the people who are in it. Right now, Krystal is working with people with a sincere desire to help and a deep understanding of how their program works. When we have meetings with Tammy (Bureau of Services for the Visually Impaired) or Jackie (small business services), I walk out knowing that

I can believe everything they told me. That's not always the case. Sometimes you leave wondering what was actually true.

The lesson here is that you can't discount an agency just because it doesn't always work out. The outcome for different situations can change based on who you are working with. Whether you get what you want can be based on funding at a given time. There are so many variables, and nothing ever seems to be set in stone.

Be flexible, and try to understand the people you are working with. Realize that your mood can also determine what you hear. A good rule of thumb is to not make rash decisions or say things you might regret. The passage of a day or two will make things seem different and affect your response.

I try to never say anything to my husband in anger. I've learned that he has a memory like a steel trap. He can tell you exactly what I said on any given date and probably whether the stock market was up or down that day. If I'm not completely sure I'm going to stick by a statement for life, I try not to say anything that I'll have to defend later when I may not be so angry.

Use that same strategy with agencies and the people in them.

Chapter Fourteen

Adult Services

There are lots of protections in IDEA. Schools require that the people who interact with your child have a certain degree of training. To get funding, there are things they are required to do.

The adult system doesn't seem to be quite as strict. Some of the people who work in those systems don't have to have the level of education that is required in the school systems. (That's how it works in the state where I live. This may differ in other states.)

I've had to deal with educational issues and rights of persons with disabilities in that setting most of my working life. I know that system and feel comfortable talking about it. Not so with adult systems. Not only are your children suddenly adults (when did that happen?) but also you, as a parent, don't have the final say anymore. Scary, huh?

In adult systems, it's not about being required to be in a program. Clients can change programs or leave them completely. They have individual service plans, not IEPs. It's not about teaching anymore. They have adult rights but not necessarily the adult skills to deal with those rights.

You could write a whole book about this. I believe disabled adults do have rights, and I try to allow them to exercise those rights. My girls still live at home, so we say what our parents used to say to us: "Our house, our rules." When I was living at home with my parents at the age of twenty-two, I had to abide by their rules. It was their home, and I respected their rules.

My husband says that they have rights, but so do all the other people around them, and they need to respect other people's rights while they're asserting their own. There's a fine line that can be hard to define. I'm sure we could have endless debates over it.

There are zealots in any movement who will take a right and push it as far as they can. Truth be told, the whole issue gives me a headache. Each individual and his or her disability is different, so I don't believe there are hard-and-fast rules for the entire community of persons with disabilities.

For example, if a person with Tourette's syndrome, who may randomly shout obscenities or rude remarks as a result of his or her disability, is not corrected in a group setting, is it acceptable for people with other disabilities to also shout obscenities? Can the person without Tourette's syndrome be taught that it is unacceptable, or is it because of their disability that they can't understand that it's wrong? Confusing, isn't it? Where do you draw the line?

These rights can play a huge part in the services disabled people receive as adults. If a workshop has rules of behavior and a client doesn't like them, the client can quit and go to another workshop. If the goal is to get them outside employment, some behaviors wouldn't be tolerated in the outside world.

There seems to be a catch-22 whereby agencies that provide workshop services can't win. Sometimes I believe they can't require stricter rules of conduct because of the diverse population they serve.

Chapter Fifteen

A Snapshot of Kim

This chapter is just to let you know a little bit more about Kim. I'm starting off with a few short pieces I wrote about her over the years.

I Want to Ride a Bike

My older daughter, Kim, age ten, was recently evaluated by occupational and physical therapists who said she would never be able to coordinate her hands, eyes, and feet to be able to ride a bicycle.

My gut instinct told me that this must be a mistake. I thought about it off and on for almost a year. The idea of getting her a bicycle grew and really took root. So for her birthday this June, I took the plunge and bought her a bicycle.

She pushed it around for a few days and sat on it a lot. She even put her feet on the pedals. I knew I had to provide some incentive, so we took the show on the road. (Literally! Of course, we do live on a dirt road.) The going was tough. She just wasn't sure she could trust herself. I pushed a bit, and she finally began to pedal. And then she was off! Talk about a proud little girl! Talk about a proud mother!

This was one of those times when I really felt strongly that the professionals might be wrong. I have to say that the day she was evaluated, though, I could see why they came to the conclusions they did.

But one factor was missing: incentive. With incentive, our kids can do things tests say they can't. If we can make them want to do something, they'll find a way. We just have to find the incentive to make them want to try hard enough. Kim is now a fairly decent rider. My instinct paid off. I just have one tiny problem. See, I also bought a bicycle for her younger sister, Krystal, who is blind. (Call me an optimist!) How do I get Kim to act as a guide for Krystal? There isn't much of a seed for incentive to grow there, but I can't keep running alongside for too much longer!

Dreams

A dream is not necessarily a full-blown vision of what a
parent wants for a child.
It may only be a tiny slice of their future life—
a moment in time:
Krystal crossing the street in a big city with her seeing-eye
dog (alone).
Krystal listening to an audiotape of a book I've read.
Kim at a school dance with friends.
It is the professional's job to see beyond the nine-month
commitment they may have with a particular child
and help the parent see how what they're doing at this
point in time will help to make that dream a reality.

I wrote that for a presentation several years ago. I happened to come across it one day last week. As I read it, I realized that my dream for

Kim to attend a school dance with friends had occurred not once, but twice since school started in September.

Now when she went to her first dance, I was a bit skeptical. But we've been working on building a circle of friends for her for the past several years. She has some pretty neat friends, and a lot of kids speak to her when we're out in public. So I'd asked one of them to watch her at the dance and help her with her money. Kim was a little timid about going into the dance, but when she saw her friends, she decided she'd stay. Her dad and I came home after dropping her off, and we both acted as if it was the most natural thing in the world. Neither of us voiced our concerns aloud. We went to pick her up, and all the kids and teachers told us what a good time she'd had and how well she'd behaved. It was a pretty big landmark for us.

Even though we realized we'd accomplished something here, we didn't place too much importance to it. When I read what I'd written though, it brought back all the memories of how she'd been when I'd written it. At that time, I really thought it would be one of those events that would never occur, but I'd still had a vision of it happening. I'm sure many of her former teachers also thought it would never happen either.

Kim is autistic. She used to run out into the road chasing butterflies, eat glass, bang her head on the wall, and hide under tables. I used to have to use the mixer and vacuum when she was asleep. Fire drills would literally send her up the wall, and she never used to play with kids—just beside them. She had some pretty severe behaviors. The thought of her actually being away from me with other kids, at a place like a dance, for any period of time was unthinkable.

Kim is now twelve years old, and I've been talking about what she might be able to do as an adult. I want her to be independent, have a job, and live a full life. To be honest, though, I have these horrible visions of where she may end up living and what she may end up having to do when I'm gone. I talk about her future, but do I think she'll be able to have a good one? Well, now that I've seen my dream about the dance come true, I can finally move on to my next dream and be able to really believe that it will come true.

As I read that story, I realize that if I hadn't written my dream down, I still wouldn't be able to fully believe in my next dream. We tend to forget how far our children have come because it's such a slow process. Perhaps its too painful to remember the past. I don't usually like going back and remembering all those things. This time was different, though. I was able to see how far she's come, and believe me, that was a good feeling. Remember to celebrate your children's successes and dream some impossible dreams. Write them down somewhere, and read them every so often. And aim high, because it's not impossible.

Kim continues to amaze us, and at the same time, frustrate us. She made some pretty remarkable progress while she was growing up. There was one summer she made so much progress that we actually thought we'd cured her. I don't know what we did, but we were never able to duplicate it. The truth is that she has probably reached her highest level. But that's okay. I can always wish for more, but at some point, you have to stop beating yourself over the head and move on. About the only thing we can do with her is to reinforce the good traits she does have. Since she is a creature of habit and fixed rules, it's not too hard to do.

Plus, Kim is content where she is. I really can't ask for more considering the progress she has made.

You do have to be very careful when you're teaching her anything new. If you make a mistake telling her how to do something, she'll continue to make that same mistake over and over, and it's sometimes nearly impossible to correct it.

Kim sings beautifully, and she sings a lot. But if she misunderstands a word in a song and sings it her way a time or two, she absolutely won't change to the correct word, no matter how many times you tell her what the right word is.

If we go back to her literal thinking, there's always the problem of what you say in any given situation. For example, she came home one time and said something inappropriate. When I tried to tell her that wasn't very nice, she told me that another person at work said that all the time. I did what we all do at times. I used one of my Dad's old sayings (one I heard quite frequently while growing up!) and said, "I don't care what so-and-so says. I don't care what they do. If they jumped off a cliff, would you jump off too?"

What Kim got from that was that I didn't like that person. She went to work the next day and told everyone that I didn't like that person. The only way I found out about it was when a staff member told me that I should watch what I said around her because she was coming to work and repeating it.

We worked a long time on that concept. I still don't think she fully understands that you can like a person but still not like everything they do or say.

We will probably always struggle with certain concepts. Kim is now twenty-seven. She has a boyfriend, but still lives at home with us. I had major dreams about how independent she would eventually become that haven't panned out. She will always need someone to help her with major decisions. It's a worry, but she is also happy where she is. I don't think we can do anymore than reinforce the good skills she does have.

Chapter Sixteen

A Snapshot of Krystal

I 'll begin this chapter with a few articles I wrote about Krystal.

A Letter to God

Dear God,

Never let it be said that I won't admit it when I'm wrong or that I never apologize to people when I should. And I have been wrong about you. I thought you'd made a terrible mistake when my child was born, and I said some pretty rotten things to you and about you. It seemed so unfair, though. I couldn't believe that you'd given me this child. I was sure you'd made a horrendous mistake, and I'm sure you got pretty tired of me begging for a miracle in one breath and then turning around and saying all those mean things about you in the next breath. I'm truly sorry.

I thought my view of the whole situation was right and yours was wrong. I doubted your wisdom, and yes, I even cursed you for doing what you did. Inexcusable, I know. But you have to realize that when she was born, I wasn't nearly the person I am now. In those days, you could have bet me a million dollars that I never would be capable of handling everything. (And even though I'm apologizing now, didn't you sometimes doubt your decision?) Anyway, you were right. This child has changed my life. She's made me be all that I'm capable of and more than I ever imagined I could be. She's made me see things I would have overlooked before.

Take this compassion thing. Yeah, I knew what the word meant, and I really thought I was compassionate back then, but I turned away when I saw a person with a disability. Sometimes, I even stared when I thought no one was watching. What a jerk I was. My brand of compassion was more like pity for all that they weren't, and I never saw them for all they were. I thought I was being truly compassionate. Thanks for teaching me otherwise.

Then there was that tolerance thing. Sure, I thought people with disabilities should have equal rights and opportunities, but would I have gone out of my way to make sure that happened? Probably not. Now I live with a person I expect others to be tolerant of. Makes you realize how tolerant you really were before and helps you to understand where other people are coming from.

And the minority thing. Coming from a white, middle-class background doesn't even begin to prepare you for all the prejudices and oppression that you face when you become a minority yourself via your child. Talk about a learning experience! It makes you empathize with all minorities.

Now I have to thank you for all the things you've taken away from me. Pettiness is one of them. When I think of all the things I used to worry about, I realize what a waste of time and energy that was. But I have to remember how I was and how I am now. Those who haven't experienced what I have won't know the difference, and with all I've learned, I have to remember how I used to feel when I dealt with them. I have to remember to understand.

Monetary things are next. I recently listened to a speaker at a conference, and one of the questions she asked was, "If given the choice, would you choose $30 million or peace and happiness?" I was in a room with close to thirty parents who had children with disabilities, and not a one of them raised their hand for the money. (Although I briefly thought that all that cash would buy some quality child care and help further the cause for equality.) However, I did realize that it wouldn't make my daughter see, nor would it replace things many other children needed. Ten years ago, I would have been convinced that the money was my answer to happiness. Now, it's secondary to what is really important.

I know now that all the times I accused you of deserting me, you were in fact carrying me, just as the *Footprints* poem says. I also know that the bad times are what helped me to grow, so I don't take them so personally now. But just so you'll realize that I'm still me and that I'm still going to need a little help (and since I've apologized so nicely), could you give me a small miracle and make my little girl see? Well, if you can't, I guess I understand. Miracles might be in short supply today, but just for the record, thanks again for letting me see. Amen.
(I wrote the above letter to God many years ago, but it still applies.)

And Krystal Wants to Be a Painter

My younger daughter, who is seven years old and blind, announced today that she wants to be a painter when she grows up. My first reaction was that all too familiar gut-wrenching, sick feeling I get when the realization that she really is blind hits me. I didn't have the heart to tell her she couldn't be a painter because she was blind.

I wandered around the house, more or less moping about the whole thing, when it struck me that a painter isn't necessarily a painter, as in still life or portrait pictures. She could be a painter who painted in textures. She could create her impression of the world in textures or whatever she chose.

Here I am, thinking I'm one of the world's biggest advocates for normal lives for special kids, falling into the stereotypical trap of what people can and cannot do. Since I've been doing some serious thinking about how to convince both of my children's teachers that they're more normal than abnormal, the irony of what had just happened was significant.

The ingrained and learned prejudices don't go away just because of one incident or even a dozen. They are so deeply embedded in us that some of the decisions we make aren't necessarily based on our new awareness of the world of disabilities. If I, a parent, can forget about the need to be creative and innovative, how can I expect her teacher not to forget?

As parents, we have to have ongoing communication with those who teach our children and share our ideas with them. We also have to stay on our toes and try not to fall back into the same old traps of setting limits on what our children can do.

I am sometimes amazed at many of the strategies my friends come up with when they interact with my children. They do things and explain things differently from how I would, but it works. I think parents can get so involved that they can't always see the forest for the trees. We're so involved with our kids that we tend to overlook major areas.

Once I realized how mistaken I'd been about my first reaction, I mentally kicked myself and went back into the living room to tell her that she could be a painter. In fact, she could be anything she wants to be with a little imagination.

Later the same evening, as I was giving her father a haircut, Krystal said she wanted to learn to cut his hair. I didn't say no, but I will have to give this one some serious thought. But, hey, it's his hair!

As I read this story, Krystal is now twenty-six. She works at a workshop during the week. It's a small workshop, and she mostly shreds paper for them.

She has a boyfriend who lives out of state. He's also visually impaired, and he's been here to visit. Although he's also blind, he has an entirely different set of skills than she does. I think they make a good team. We will see where that goes!

Krystal has always wanted to be a DJ. Years ago, we were told that would be impossible. We were able to buy her professional speakers and an amp and some other pieces of equipment from a friend. Don't ask me what all she has. I know what to plug in and where to plug it in. Anyway, she's been a DJ a couple of times at small events, but she is working a real wedding reception next month.

She has also been working with the Bureau of Services for the Visually Impaired and is likely to be receiving some assistance from them to set up her own business spinning and preparing yarn and other products. We have a herd of llamas, so we have our own fiber to work with.

It's been an exciting year for her, and I believe she has a bright future. She still requires a great deal of help from us, but one day, she should be able to do this and employ others to help with the things she can't do.

What she needs most at this time in her life is experience with life. She has to learn that things can't always be her way and that the world isn't always a nice place. Due to her visual impairment, she's socially immature about many things. It's because she hasn't had the opportunity to be out in the world of her sighted peers.

I'm glad about some of those things she hasn't been able to experience, but it makes her too trusting. I still don't think she knows there are bad people who will take advantage of her. Her dad and I try to explain those things, but I think she's at the age where she thinks we are really stupid.

She and I share a good friend who is also visually impaired. He gives her advice about relationships that I can't. I explained about the birds and the bees. Isn't that all a mother is required to do?

Could be worse though, couldn't it? We still have many challenges to overcome.

But they're just little hills, not big mountains.

Chapter Seventeen

In Conclusion

There are so many things that come to mind that haven't fit into any of the subjects I've discussed. My life has been a series of incidents that have occurred over many years with my children. Sometimes, these incidents lean toward a very specific topic, and other times, they are simply incidents that don't seem to fit any topic. I could go on and on to tell you about them, but it would be more rambling than anything else.

I have been fortunate to have the opportunity to work with so many people in so many situations. The one thing I have learned is that there is no right way for everyone. There are so many variables that go into any situation, and in the end, you simply have to do what is best for you. You are the one who has to go to bed at night and feel that you have done the right thing for you and for your child. You may not be the most popular parent in your school system, but being liked doesn't necessarily provide the best outcome for your child.

You may not have agreed with everything I've written, and that's okay. I don't expect you to. We are all individuals, and we all have our own ways of dealing with issues. Be strong in your conviction of who you are, and remember that you are not alone.